LEON TROTSKY

Whither France?

merit publishers

873 Broadway
New York, N.Y. 10003

 126

MERIT PUBLISHERS
873 Broadway
New York, N.Y. 10003

Translated by John G. Wright and Harold R. Isaacs
Copyright 1936 by Pioneer Publishers
Copyright © 1968 by Merit Publishers

LIBRARY OF CONGRESS Catalog Card Number: 68-54537

ALL RIGHTS RESERVED
PRINTED IN THE UNITED STATES OF AMERICA

CONTENTS

Publisher's Note

The tumultuous events in France during May and June of 1968 present many significant parallels with the social and political crisis generated by the mass strikes of May—June 1936 in that same country.

Then, as now, millions of workers went on strike and paralyzed the nation's economy. Their occupation of the factories and raising of the red flag as the symbol of the better world they hoped to build, along with the support and sympathy they received from other sectors of the people, squarely posed the question of power. Which class was going to rule France?

Then, as today, the Communist Party and Social Democratic leaderships acted to restrain the gigantic mass movement from making the most of the exceptionally favorable opportunity to get rid of capitalism and establish a workers' republic.

In 1936—1937 the Popular Front coalition of the reformist and Stalinist parties with the left bourgeoisie derailed the working-class offensive, enabled the shaken propertied interests to catch their breath, and helped reaction to stage a comeback.

The present generation of militant workers and rebellious students who are combating de Gaulle's authoritarianism have the lessons of that bitter experience in mind. They are striving to prevent the Stalinist and reformist misleaders from carrying through their betrayal to the end in 1968 as in 1936.

The similarities in the two situations fully warrant the timely republication of this compilation of articles written by Leon Trotsky in France and Norway from November 1934 to June 1936. In these incisive and prophetic pages, the exiled revolutionist pointed to the collapse of the old political mechanism through which the French bourgeoisie wielded its power, stressed the necessity for an extra-parliamentary struggle against the threat of Bonapartism, and sketched out a program of action which could lead to victory for the socialist revolution.

The ideas he put forward at that time have not lost an iota of their actuality.

June 12, 1968

Preface

THIS PAMPHLET contains several articles written at different times during the past two and a half years; or to put it more accurately, from the emergence of the Fascist-Bonapartist-Royalist bloc on February 6, 1934 to the great mass strike of May-June, 1936. What a vast swing of the political pendulum! The leaders of the People's Front are of course inclined to credit the foresight and wisdom of their policies for the swing to the Left that has taken place. But that is not the case. The three-party cartel proved to be a third rate factor in the development of the political crisis. The Communists, Socialists and Radicals foresaw nothing and directed nothing. Events broke over their heads. The unexpected (for them) blow of February 6, 1934 compelled them to ditch yesterday's slogans and ideas and to seek salvation in an alliance with each other. Equally unexpected, the strike of May-June 1936 has dealt this parliamentary bloc a blow from which it cannot recover. That which superficially might seem to be the apogee of the People's Front is in reality its dying agony.

In view of the fact that the various sections of this pamphlet appeared separately, reflecting the different stages of the crisis through which France was passing, the reader will find unavoidable repetitions in these pages. To eliminate them would mean to dislocate the structure of each section and, what is more important, would strip the work of its dynamic character, which reflects the dynamics of the events themselves. The author has chosen to retain these repetitions. They may even prove not entirely without use for the reader. We live in an epoch of the universal liquidation of Marxism in the ruling summits of the labor movement. The most vulgar prejudices now serve as the official doctrines for the political and trade union leaders of the French working class. Contrariwise, the voice of revolutionary realism rings against this artificial sounding board like the voice of "sectarianism." It is all the more insistently necessary *to repeat over and over again* the fundamental truths of Marxist policies before audiences of advanced workers.

Here, or in other occasional statements of the author, the reader may perhaps find isolated contradictions. We do not eliminate these either. In fact, these supposed "contradictions" reflect only the emphasis placed on different sides of the same phenomenon at different stages of the process. On the whole, we think this pamphlet has passed the test of events and, it may be, will prove capable of making them more readily understood.

The days of the great strike will undoubtedly also have the merit of airing out the musty, still atmosphere of the workers' organizations, clearing it of the miasmas of reformism and patriotism, of the "Socialist," "Communist" and "trade union" varieties. Assuredly, this will not take place at once, nor by itself. Ahead lies a stubborn ideological struggle on the basis of harsh class struggle. But the subsequent course of the crisis will show that only Marxism provides a timely analysis of the inter-locking of events and a timely forecast of their further development.

The February days of 1934 marked the first serious offensive of the united counter-revolution. The May-June days of 1936 herald the first mighty wave of proletarian revolution. These two milestones show the way in advance to two possible roads: the Italian or the Russian. Parliamentary democracy, in whose name the Blum government now functions, will be crushed into powder between these two great millstones. Whatever the specific stages to come, the transitional combinations and groupings, the partial attacks and retreats, the tactical episodes, there henceforth remains the choice only between Fascism and the proletarian revolution. That is the meaning of this book.

LEON TROTSKY.

June 10, 1936.

1

Whither France?

1. The Collapse of Bourgeois Democracy

After the war a series of brilliantly victorious revolutions
occurred in Russia, Germany, Austria-Hungary and later
in Spain. But it was only in Russia that the proletariat
took full power into its hands, expropriated its exploiters,
and knew how to create and maintain a Workers' State.
Everywhere else the proletariat, despite its victory, stopped
half way because of the mistakes of its leadership. As a
result, power slipped from its hands, shifted from Left to
Right and fell prey to Fascism. In a series of other countries
power passed into the hands of a military dictatorship.
Nowhere were the parliaments capable of reconciling class
contradictions and assuring the peaceful development of
events. Conflicts were solved arms in hand.

The French people for a long time thought that Fascism
had nothing whatever to do with them. They had a republic
in which all questions were dealt with by the sovereign people
through the exercise of universal suffrage. But on February
6, 1934, several thousand Fascists and Royalists, armed
with revolvers, clubs and razors, imposed upon the country
the reactionary government of Doumergue, under whose
protection the Fascist bands continue to grow and arm themselves. What does tomorrow hold?

Of course in France, as in certain other European countries (England, Belgium, Holland, Switzerland, the Scandi-
navian countries), there still exist parliaments, elections,
democratic liberties, or their remnants. But in all these

7

countries the class struggle is sharpening, just as it did previously in Italy and Germany. Whoever consoles himself with the phrase, "France is not Germany," is hopeless. In all countries the same historic laws operate, the laws of capitalist decline. If the means of production remain in the hands of a small number of capitalists, there is no way out for society. It is condemned to go from crisis to crisis, from need to misery, from bad to worse. In the various countries the decrepitude and disintegration of capitalism are expressed in diverse forms and at unequal rhythms. But the basic features of the process are the same everywhere. *The bourgeoisie is leading its society to complete bankruptcy.* It is capable of assuring the people neither bread nor peace. *This is precisely why it cannot any longer tolerate the democratic order.* It is forced to smash the workers by the use of physical violence. The discontent of the workers and peasants, however, cannot be brought to an end by the police alone. Moreover, it is often impossible to make the army march against the people. It begins by disintegrating and ends with the passage of a large section of the soldiers over to the people's side. That is why finance capital is obliged to create special armed bands, trained to fight the workers just as certain breeds of dog are trained to hunt game. The historic function of Fascism is to smash the working class, destroy its organizations, and stifle political liberties when the capitalists find themselves unable to govern and dominate with the help of democratic machinery.

The Fascists find their human material mainly in the petty bourgeoisie. The latter has been entirely ruined by big capital. There is no way out for it in the present social order, but it knows of no other. Its dissatisfaction, indignation and despair are diverted by the Fascists away from big capital and against the workers. It may be said that Fascism is the act of placing the petty bourgeoisie at the disposal of its most bitter enemies. In this way big capital ruins the middle classes and then with the help of hired Fascist demagogues incites the despairing petty bourgeois against the worker. The bourgeois regime can be preserved only by such murderous means as these. For how long? Until it is overthrown by proletarian revolution.

2. THE BEGINNING OF BONAPARTISM IN FRANCE

In France the movement from democracy toward Fascism is only in its first stage. Parliament exists, but it no longer has the powers it once had and it will never retrieve them. The parliamentary majority, mortally frightened after February 6, called to power Doumergue, the savior, the arbiter. His government holds itself above Parliament. It bases itself not on the "democratically" elected majority but directly and immediately upon the bureaucratic apparatus, the police and the army. This is precisely why Doumergue can permit no liberty for the civil servants or in general for employees of the state. He needs a docile and disciplined bureaucratic apparatus on whose summit he can maintain himself without danger of falling. The parliamentary majority, scared of the Fascists and the "common front," is forced to bow before Doumergue.

At the present time much is being written about the forthcoming "reform" of the Constitution, on the right to dissolve the Chamber of Deputies, etc. All these questions have only a juridical interest. In the political sense, the question is already solved. Reform has been accomplished without the trip to Versailles.* The appearance on the arena of armed Fascist bands has enabled finance capital to raise itself above Parliament. In this consists now the essence of the French Constitution. All else is illusion, phraseology or conscious dupery.

The present role of Doumergue (like that of his possible successors, of the type of Tardieu) is nothing new. It is a role analogous to that played, in different circumstances,

* Under French parliamentary procedure, constitutional reforms are considered by a joint session of the Chamber and Senate, convening at Versailles.—TR.

by Napoleon I and Napoleon III. The essence of Bonapartism consists in this: basing itself on the struggle of
two camps, it "saves" the "nation" with the help of a
bureaucratic-military dictatorship. Napoleon I represented
the Bonapartism of the bourgeoisie's impetuous youth. The
Bonapartism of Napoleon III developed when the bourgeoisie was already slightly bald. In the person of Doumergue we meet the senile Bonapartism of capitalist decline.

The Doumergue Government represents the first step of
the passage from parliamentarianism to Bonapartism. To
keep his balance, Doumergue needs at his right hand the
Fascist and other bands which brought him to power. To
demand of him that he dissolve the Patriotic Youth, the
Croix de Feu, the Camelots du Roi, etc.—not on paper but
in reality—is to demand that he cut off the branch upon
which he rests.

Temporary oscillations to one side or the other are, of
course, possible. Thus, a premature Fascist offensive might
provoke a certain shift to the "Left" at the top of the government. Doumergue would temporarily give way not to
Tardieu but to Herriot. But in the first place, no one has
ever said that the Fascists would attempt a premature *coup
d'état*. Secondly, a temporary shift to the Left at the top
would not change the general course of development. It
would only postpone the showdown.

There is no longer any path back to a peaceful democracy. Events are leading inevitably and irresistibly to a
conflict between the proletariat and Fascism.

3. Will Bonapartism Last Long?

How long can the present transitional Bonapartist regime
stand? Or in other words: how much time has the proletariat to prepare itself for the decisive battle? To this
question it is impossible, naturally, to give an exact reply.
But certain factors can be established for the purposes of
evaluating the tempo at which the whole process is develop-

ing. For this the foremost element is the question of the immediate fate of the *Radical Party.*

The very appearance of the present Bonapartist regime links it, as we have said, to the beginning of a civil war between the extreme political camps. It finds its principal material support in the police and the army. But it also has a political support on the Left—the Radical Socialist Party. The base of this mass party is in the petty bourgeoisie of town and country. Its summit is occupied by "democratic" agents of the big bourgeoisie of town and country who have given the people occasional small reforms and more often democratic phrases, who have saved it daily (in words) from reaction and clericalism, but who, in all important questions, have carried out the policy of big capital.

Under the threat of Fascism, and still more under the threat of the proletariat, the Radical Socialists have found themselves obliged to pass from the camp of parliamentary "democracy" over to the camp of Bonapartism. Like the camel under its driver's whip, Radicalism gets down on its four knees to let capitalist reaction sit between its humps. Without the political support of the Radicals, the Doumergue government would at the present moment be impossible.

If the political evolution of France is compared with that of Germany, the Doumergue government and its possible successors correspond to the Brüning, Papen and Schleicher governments which filled in the gap between Weimar and Hitler. There is, however, a difference which, politically, *can* assume enormous importance. German Bonapartism came upon the scene when the democratic parties had collapsed and the Nazis were growing at a prodigious rate. The three Bonapartist governments in Germany, having a very feeble base of their own, were balanced on the tight rope stretched across the abyss between two hostile camps —*the proletariat and Fascism.* All three of these governments fell quickly. The camp of the proletariat was split

11

and unprepared for the struggle, disoriented, duped and betrayed by its leaders. The Nazis were able to take power almost without a struggle.

French Fascism does not yet represent a mass force. On the other hand, Bonapartism finds support, neither sure nor very stable but nevertheless a mass support, in the Radicals. Between these two facts there is an inner link. By the social character of its base, Radicalism is the party of the petty bourgeoisie. Fascism can only become a mass force by conquering the petty bourgeoisie. In other words, *Fascism can develop in France above all at the expense of the Radicals*. This process is already under way, although still in its early stages.

4. THE ROLE OF THE RADICAL PARTY

The last district elections gave results which could and should have been anticipated. The flanks, i.e., the reactionaries and the workers' bloc, gained and the center, i.e., the Radicals, lost. But gains and losses are still negligible. If it were a question of parliamentary elections, these phenomena would have undoubtedly taken on much more considerable dimensions. The displacements which have been noted have for us an importance not in themselves but only as symptoms of changes in the consciousness of the masses.

They show that the petty bourgeois center has already begun to give way to the two extreme camps. That means that the remnants of the parliamentary regime are going to be increasingly eaten away. The extreme camps are going to grow. Clashes between them are approaching. It is not difficult to understand that this process is absolutely inescapable.

The Radical Party is the party with whose aid the big bourgeoisie preserves the hopes of the petty bourgeoisie in a progressive and peaceful improvement of its situation. This role of the Radicals was possible only so long as the economic situation of the petty bourgeoisie remained supportable and tolerable, so long as mass ruin was averted, so long as the petty bourgeoisie retained its hope in the future. To be sure, the program of the Radicals has always remained on paper. They have brought about no serious social reform in behalf of the toilers nor could they have done so. It was not permitted by the big bourgeoisie which holds on to all the real levers of power, the banks and the Bourse, the press, the higher officials, key diplomats and the general staff.

From time to time the Radicals handed out petty alms to their clientele, especially on a provincial scale, and, with the help of these hand-outs, preserved the illusions of the popular masses. Thus it went until the last crisis. It has now become clear to the most backward peasant that it is not a matter of an ordinary, passing crisis, of which there were not a few before the war, but of a crisis of the whole social system. It calls for bold, decisive measures. What ones? The peasant does not know. No one has told him what he should have been told.

Capitalism has brought the means of production to such a level that they are paralyzed by the misery of the popular masses, ruined by the selfsame capitalism. The whole system has thereby begun to decline, decompose, and rot. Capitalism not only cannot give the toilers new social re-forms, nor even petty alms. It is forced to take back what it once gave. All of Europe has entered an era of economic and political counter-reforms. The policy of despoiling and suffocating the masses stems not from the caprices of the reaction but from the decomposition of the capitalist sys-tem. That is the fundamental fact which must be assimilated by every worker if he is not to be duped by hollow phrases.

That is precisely why the democratic reformist parties are disintegrating and losing their forces one after another throughout Europe. The same fate also awaits the French Radicals. Only fools can think that the capitulation of Daladier or the treason of Herriot in the face of the worst reaction results from fortuitous, temporary causes or from

the lack of character in these two lamentable leaders. No!
Great political phenomena always have profound social
causes. The decline of the democratic parties is a universal
phenomenon whose causes rest in the disintegration of capitalism itself. The big bourgeoisie says to the Radicals:
"Now is no time for joking. If you do not stop flirting with
the socialists and coyly promising the people mountains and
miracles, I will call in the Fascists. Understand that February 6 was only a first warning!" After which the Radical
camel gets down on his four knees. There is nothing else
he can do.

But Radicalism will not find its salvation along that road.
Linking its fate in the eyes of the people to the fate of the
reaction, it inevitably hastens its own end. The loss of
votes and mandates in the district elections is only a beginning. The process of the collapse of the Radical Party will
unfold with increasing speed. The whole question is to know
in whose favor this inevitable and irresistible collapse will
take place—in favor of the proletarian revolution or Fascism.

Will it be revolutionary Socialism or Fascist reaction
which will first offer the middle classes, boldly and broadly,
the most convincing program and, what is the most important, win their confidence by demonstrating in words and
deeds its ability to smash every obstacle on the road to a
better future?

On this question depends the fate of France for many
years to come. Not only of France, but of all Europe. Not
only of Europe, but of the entire world.

5. The "Middle Classes," the Radical Party
and Fascism

Since the victory of the Nazis in Germany there has been
much talk in the parties and groups of the French "Left"
of the necessity for staying close to the "middle classes" to
bar the road to Fascism. The fraction of Renaudel and Co.
split from the Socialist Party for the particular purpose

of drawing near to the Radicals. But at the moment that
Renaudel, who lives on the ideas of 1848, extended both
hands to Herriot, the latter had both his engaged, the one
by Tardieu, the other by Louis Marin.

From this, however, it does not at all follow that the
working class can turn its back on the petty bourgeoisie,
leaving it to its fate. Oh, no! To approach the peasants
and the petty bourgeoisie of the cities, to draw them to our
side, is the necessary condition of the success of the struggle
against Fascism, not to speak of the conquest of power.
Only the problem must be correctly posed, and for that it is
necessary to understand clearly the nature of the "middle
classes." Nothing is more dangerous in politics, especially
in a critical period, than to repeat general formulas without
examining their social content.

Contemporary society is composed of three classes: the
big bourgeoisie, the proletariat and the "middle classes,"
or the petty bourgeoisie. The relations among these three
classes determine in the final analysis the political situation
in the country. The fundamental classes of society are the
big bourgeoisie and the proletariat. Only these two classes
can have a clear, consistent, independent policy of their
own. The petty bourgeoisie is distinguished by its economic
dependence and its social heterogeneity. Its upper stratum
is linked directly to the big bourgeoisie. Its lower stratum
merges with the proletariat and even falls to the status of
lumpen-proletariat. In accordance with its economic situation, the petty bourgeoisie can have no policy of its own. It
always oscillates between the capitalists and the workers.
Its own upper stratum pushes it to the Right; its lower
strata, oppressed and exploited, are capable in certain conditions of turning sharply to the Left. These contradictory
relations among the different strata of the "middle classes"
always determine the confused and thoroughly bankrupt
policy of the Radicals, their vacillations between the cartel
with the Socialists to calm the base and the national bloc
with the capitalist reaction to save the bourgeoisie. *The*

*final decomposition of Radicalism begins when the big bour-
geoisie, itself in an impasse, permits it to vacillate no longer.*

The petty bourgeoisie, the ruined masses of city and
country, begins to lose patience. It assumes an attitude
more and more hostile towards its own upper stratum. It
becomes convinced of the bankruptcy and the perfidy of its
political leadership. The poor peasant, the artisan, the
petty merchant become convinced that an abyss separates
them from all these mayors, all these lawyers and political
businessmen of the type of Herriot, Daladier, Chautemps
and Co., who by their mode of life and their conceptions
are big bourgeois. It is precisely this disillusionment of the
petty bourgeoisie, its impatience, its despair, that Fascism
exploits. Its agitators stigmatize and execrate the parliamentary democracy which supports careerists and grafters
but gives nothing to the toilers. These demagogues shake
their fists at the bankers, the big merchants and the capitalists. Their words and gestures correspond to the feelings of
the small proprietors bogged up a blind alley. The Fascists
show boldness, go out into the streets, attack the police,
and attempt to drive out Parliament by force. That makes
an impression on the despairing petty bourgeois. He says
to himself: "The Radicals, among whom there are too many
swindlers, have definitely sold themselves to the bankers; the
Socialists have promised for a long time to abolish exploitation but they never pass from words to deeds; the Communists one cannot understand at all—today it is one thing,
tomorrow another; let's see if the Fascists cannot save us."

6. Must the "Middle Classes" Inevitably Go
Over to Fascism?

Renaudel, Frossard and their similars imagine that the
petty bourgeoisie is attached above all to democracy, where-
fore it is necessary to hang on to the coat-tails of the
Radicals. What monstrous confusion! Democracy is only
a political form. The petty bourgeoisie is not concerned

with the shell but with the kernel. It wants to save itself from misery and ruin. If democracy proves impotent—then to the devil with democracy! Every petty bourgeois reasons or feels this way.

The principal social and political source of Fascism is in the growing revolt of the lower petty bourgeoisie against its own, "educated" upper layers in the municipalities, the districts and in Parliament. To this must be added the hatred of the crisis-shattered intellectual youth for the lawyers, the deputies and the parvenu ministers. Here also the lower petty bourgeois intellectuals rebel against those above them.

Does this mean that the passage of the petty bourgeoisie to Fascism is inevitable and inescapable? No, such a conclusion would be shameful fatalism.

What is really inevitable and inescapable is the doom of Radicalism and all the political groupings which link themselves to its fate.

Under conditions of capitalist decline there is no longer any place for a party of democratic reforms and "peaceful" progress. Whatever path events take in France, Radicalism will disappear from the scene, rejected and dishonored by the petty bourgeoisie which it has definitely betrayed.

Every conscious worker will become convinced by the experience of every passing day that our prediction corresponds to reality. New elections will bring defeats for the Radicals. Whole sections will cut away one after another, the popular masses below and groups of frightened careerists above. Departures, splits, betrayals will follow uninterruptedly. No maneuver nor any bloc will save the Radical Party. It will draw into the abyss with it the "party" of Renaudel-Deat & Co. The end of the Radical Party is the inevitable result of the fact that bourgeois society can no longer overcome its difficulties with the help of so-called democratic methods. The split between the base of the petty bourgeoisie and its summit is inevitable.

But that does not at all mean that the masses who follow

Radicalism must *infallibly* place their hopes in Fascism. Certainly the most demoralized section, the most declassed and the most avid of the youth of the middle classes have already made their choice in that direction. It is out of this reservoir particularly that the Fascist bands are taking form. But the basic masses of city and country have not yet made their choice. They hesitate before a great decision. It is precisely because they are hesitating that they still continue, although already without confidence, to vote for the Radicals. This situation of hesitation, of irresolution, will not, however, last for years, but for months.

Political developments in the coming period will move at a febrile rhythm. The petty bourgeoisie will reject the demagogy of Fascism only if it puts its faith in the reality of another road. That other road is the road of proletarian revolution.

7. Is It True that the Petty Bourgeoisie Fears Revolution?

Parliamentary cretins who consider themselves connoisseurs of the people like to repeat: "One must not frighten the middle classes with revolution. They do not like extremes." In this general form this affirmation is absolutely false. Naturally, the petty proprietor prefers order so long as business is going well and so long as he hopes that tomorrow it will go better.

But when this hope is lost, he is easily enraged and is ready to give himself over to the most extreme measures. Otherwise, how could he have overthrown the democratic state and brought Fascism to power in Italy and Germany? The despairing petty bourgeois sees in Fascism, above all, a fighting force against big capital, and believes that, unlike the working class parties which deal only in words, Fascism will use force to establish more "justice." The peasant and the artisan are in their manner realists. They understand that one cannot forego the use of force.

WHITHER FRANCE?

It is false, thrice false, to affirm that the present petty bourgeoisie is not going to the working class parties because it fears "extreme measures." Quite the contrary. The lower petty bourgeoisie, its great masses, only see in the working class parties parliamentary machines. They do not believe in their strength, nor in their capacity to struggle, nor in their readiness this time to conduct the struggle to the end.

And if this is so, is it worth the trouble to replace Radicalism by its parliamentary confrères on the Left? That is how the semi-expropriated, ruined and discontented proprietor reasons or feels. Without an understanding of this psychology of the peasants, the artisans, the employees, the petty functionaries, etc.—a psychology which flows from the social crisis—it is impossible to elaborate a correct policy. The petty bourgeoisie is economically dependent and politically atomized. That is why it cannot conduct an independent policy. It needs a "leader" who inspires it with confidence. This individual or collective leadership, i.e., a personage or party, can be given to it by one or the other of the fundamental classes—either the big bourgeoisie or the proletariat. Fascism unites and arms the scattered masses. Out of human dust it organizes combat detachments. It thus gives the petty bourgeoisie the illusion of being an independent force. It begins to imagine that it will really command the state. It is not surprising that these illusions and hopes turn the head of the party bourgeoisie!

But the petty bourgeoisie can also find a leader in the proletariat. This was demonstrated in Russia and partially in Spain. In Italy, in Germany and in Austria the petty bourgeoisie gravitated in this direction. But the parties of the proletariat did not rise to their historic task.

To bring the petty bourgeoisie to its side, the proletariat must win its confidence. And for that it must have confidence in its own strength.

It must have a clear program of action and must be ready to struggle for power by all possible means. Tempered by its revolutionary party for a decisive and pitiless struggle, the proletariat says to the peasants and petty bourgeoisie of the cities: "We are struggling for power. Here is our program. We are ready to discuss with you changes in this program. We will employ violence only against big capital and its lackeys, but with you toilers, we desire to conclude an alliance on the basis of a given program." The peasants will understand such language. Only, they must have faith in the capacity of the proletariat to seize power.

But for that it is necessary to purge the united front of all equivocation, of all indecision, of all hollow phrases. It is necessary to understand the situation and to place oneself seriously on the revolutionary road.

8. AN ALLIANCE WITH THE RADICALS WOULD BE AN ALLIANCE AGAINST THE MIDDLE CLASSES

Renaudel, Frossard and their similars seriously imagine that an alliance with the Radicals is an alliance with the "middle classes" and consequently a barrier against Fascism. These men see nothing but parliamentary shadows. They ignore the real evolution of the masses and chase after the "Radical Party" which has outlived itself and which in the meantime turns its back on them. They think that in an era of great social crisis an alliance of classes set in motion can be replaced by a bloc with a parliamentary clique that is compromised and doomed to extinction. A real alliance of the proletariat and the middle classes is not a question of parliamentary statistics but of revolutionary dynamics.

This alliance must be created and forged in the struggle. The whole meaning of the present political situation resides in the fact that the despairing petty bourgeoisie is beginning to break from the yoke of parliamentary discipline and from the tutelage of the conservative "radical" clique which has always fooled the people, and which has now definitely betrayed it. To join in this situation with the Radicals means to condemn oneself to the scorn of the masses, and to push the petty bourgeoisie into the embrace of Fascism as the sole savior.

The working class party must occupy itself not with a hopeless effort to save the party of the bankrupts. It must, on the contrary, with all its strength, accelerate the process of liberation of the masses from Radical influence. The more zeal and the more boldness it applies to this task, the more surely and rapidly will it prepare a real alliance of the working class with the petty bourgeoisie. It is necessary to approach the classes in motion. It is necessary to place oneself at their head and not at their tail. History is working quickly. Woe to him who lags behind!

When Frossard denies the right of the Socialist Party to expose, weaken and speed the disintegration of the Radical Party, he comes forward not as a socialist but as a conservative radical. Only that party has the right to historical existence which believes in its own program and strives to rally the whole people to its banner. Otherwise it is not a party but a parliamentary coterie, a clique of careerists. It is not only the right but the elementary duty of the proletarian party to free the toiling masses from the fatal influence of the bourgeoisie. This historic task takes on a particular sharpness at the present time, for the Radicals are more than ever striving to cover up the reaction, to lull and dupe the people and in this way prepare for the victory of Fascism. And the Left Radicals? They capitulate to Herriot, just as Herriot capitulates to Tardieu.

Frossard would have the alliance of the Socialists and the Radicals end in a government of the "Left" which will dissolve the Fascist organizations and save the republic. It is difficult to imagine a more monstrous amalgam of democratic illusions and police cynicism. When we say—we speak of this in more detail below—that *what is needed is a workers' militia*, Frossard and his satellites object: "Against Fascism one must fight not with physical but with ideological means." When we say only a bold mobilization of the masses, which is only possible in a struggle against Radicalism, is capable of mining the ground under Fascism, the same gentlemen reply to us: "No, only the police government of Daladier-Frossard can save us."

What pitiful prattle! For the Radicals have held the power, and if they voluntarily ceded it to Doumergue, it was not because they lacked the aid of Frossard but because they feared Fascism, because they feared the big bourgeoisie which threatened it with Royalist razors and because they feared still more the proletariat which was beginning to marshal itself against Fascism. To cap it all, Frossard himself, taking fright at the alarm of the Radicals, advised Daladier to capitulate.

If one supposes for an instant—an obviously unlikely hypothesis—that the Radicals had consented to break the alliance with Doumergue for the alliance with Frossard, the Fascist bands, this time with the direct collaboration of the police, would have come into the streets trebly numerous, and the Radicals, together with Frossard, would have immediately crawled under the tables or hidden themselves in their ministerial toilets.

But let us make one more fantastic hypothesis: the police of Daladier-Frossard "disarm the Fascists." Does that settle the question? And who will disarm the same police, who with the right hand will give back to the Fascists what they will have taken from them with the left? The comedy of disarmament by the police will only have caused the authority of the Fascists to increase as fighters against the capitalist state. Blows against the Fascist gangs can prove effective only to the extent that these gangs are at the same time politically isolated.

Meanwhile, the hypothetical government of Daladier-Frossard would give nothing either to the workers or to the petty bourgeois masses because it would be unable to attack the foundations of private property and without expropriation of the banks, the great commercial enterprises, the key branches of industry and transport, without foreign trade monopoly, and without a series of other profound measures, there is no possible way of coming to the aid of the peasant, the artisan, the petty merchant. By its passivity, its impotence, its lies, the government of Daladier-Frossard would provoke a tempest of revolt in the petty bourgeoisie, and would push it definitely on the road to Fascism, if . . . if this government were possible. It is necessary to recognize, however, that Frossard is not alone. The same day (October 24) on which the moderate Zyromski came out in *Le Populaire* against the attempt of Frossard to revive the cartel, Cachin spoke up in *l'Humanité* to defend the idea of a bloc with the Radical Socialists. He, Cachin, greeted with enthusiasm the fact that the Radicals had declared for the "disarmament of the Fascists."

Certainly, the Radicals declared themselves for the disarmament of everyone—workers' organizations included. Certainly, in the hands of a Bonapartist state, such a measure would be directed especially against the workers. Certainly, the "disarmed" Fascists would receive on the morrow double their arms, not without the aid of the police. But why trouble with sombre reflections? Every man needs to hope. So there is Cachin travelling in the footsteps of Wels and Otto Bauer who also in their time sought salvation in the disarmament to be effected by the police of Brüning and Dollfuss.

Executing the latest turn of 180 degrees, Cachin identifies the Radicals with the middle classes. He sees oppressed peasants only through the prism of Radicalism. The alliance with the petty toiling proprietors is represented by him only in the form of a bloc with the parliamentary careerists who are at last beginning to lose the confidence of the petty proprietors.

Instead of nourishing and fanning the nascent revolt of the peasant and the artisan against the "democratic" exploiters and guiding this revolt in the direction of an alliance with the proletariat, Cachin is preparing to support the bankrupt Radicals with the authority of the "common front," and thus to drive the revolt of the most exploited petty bourgeois along the road of Fascism.

Theoretical sloppiness always takes cruel vengeance in revolutionary politics. "Anti-Fascism," like Fascism, are for the Stalinists not concrete conceptions but two great empty sacks into which they stuff anything that comes into their hands. For them Doumergue is a Fascist just as before that Daladier was also for them a Fascist. In point of fact, Doumergue is a capitalist exploiter of the Fascist wing of the petty bourgeoisie just as Herriot is an exploiter of the radical petty bourgeoisie. At the present time these two systems combine in the Bonapartist regime. Doumergue is also, after his fashion, an "anti-Fascist," since he prefers a military and police dictatorship of big capital to a civil war whose issue is always uncertain. For fear of Fascism and still more for fear of the proletariat, the "anti-Fascist" Daladier joins with Doumergue. But the regime of Doumergue is inconceivable without the existence of the Fascist gangs. An elementary Marxian analysis thus shows the utter futility of the idea of an alliance with the Radicals against Fascism!

The Radicals themselves will take pains to show in action how fantastic and reactionary are the political day dreams of Frossard and Cachin.

9. THE WORKERS' MILITIA AND ITS OPPONENTS

To struggle, it is necessary to conserve and strengthen the instrument and the means of struggle—organizations, the press, meetings, etc. Fascism threatens all of that directly and immediately. It is still too weak for the direct struggle for power but it is strong enough to attempt to beat down the working class organizations bit by bit, to temper its bands in its attacks, and to spread dismay and lack of confidence in their forces in the ranks of the workers.

Fascism finds unconscious helpers in all those who say that the "physical struggle" is impermissible or hopeless, and demand of Doumergue the disarmament of his Fascist guard. Nothing is so dangerous for the proletariat, especially in the present situation, than the sugared poison of false hopes. Nothing increases the insolence of the Fascists so much as "flabby pacifism" on the part of the workers' organizations. Nothing destroys the confidence of the middle classes in the working class as temporizing, passivity, and the absence of the will to struggle.

Le Populaire and especially *l'Humanité* write every day: "The united front is a barrier against Fascism"; "the united front will not permit . . ."; "the Fascists will not dare"; etc. These are phrases. It is necessary to say squarely to the workers, socialists, and communists: do not allow yourselves to be lulled by the phrases of superficial and irresponsible journalists and orators. It is a question of our heads and the future of socialism. It is not that we deny the importance of the united front. We demanded it when the leaders of both parties were against it. The united front opens up numerous *possibilities* but nothing more. In itself, the united front decides nothing. Only the struggle of the masses decides. The united front will reveal its value when Communist detachments will come to the help of Socialist detachments and vice versa in the case of an attack by the Fascist bands against *Le Populaire* or *l'Humanité*. But for that, proletarian combat detachments must exist and be educated, trained and armed. And if there is not an organization of defense, i.e., a workers' militia, *Le Populaire* and *l'Humanité* will be able to write as many articles as they like on the omnipotence of the united front but the two papers will find themselves defenseless before the first well prepared attack of the Fascists.

We propose to make a critical study of the "arguments" and the "theories" of the opponents of the workers' militia who are very numerous and influential in the two working class parties.

"We need mass self-defense and not the militia," we are often told. But what is this "mass self-defense" without combat organizations, without specialized cadres, without arms? To give over the defense against Fascism to unorganized and unprepared masses left to themselves would be to play a role incomparably lower than the role of Pontius Pilate. To deny the role of the militia is to deny the role of the vanguard. Then why a party? Without the support of the masses, the militia is nothing. But without organized combat detachments, the most heroic masses will be smashed bit by bit by the Fascist gangs. It is nonsense to counterpose the militia to self-defense. The militia is an organ of self-defense.

"To call for the organization of a militia," say some opponents who, to be sure, are the least serious and honest, "is to engage in provocation." This is not an argument but an insult. If the necessity for the defense of the workers' organizations flows from the whole situation, how then can one not call for the creation of the militia? Perhaps they mean to say that the creation of a militia "provokes" Fascist attacks and government repression. In that case this is an absolutely reactionary argument. Liberalism has always said to the workers that by their class struggle they "provoke" the reaction.

The reformists repeated this accusation against the Marxists, the Mensheviks against the Bolsheviks. These accusations reduced themselves, in the final analysis, to the profound thought that if the oppressed do not balk, the oppressors will not be obliged to beat them. This is the philosophy of Tolstoy and Gandhi but never that of Marx and Lenin. If *l'Humanité** wants hereafter to develop the

*In *l'Humanité* of October 30, 1934, Vaillant-Couturier proves not at all poorly that it is senseless to demand the disarming of the Fascists by the government, that only a mass movement can disarm them. Inasmuch as it is obviously a question here not of "the ideological" but physical disarmament, we trust that *l'Humanité* will now recognize the necessity of a workers' militia. We are ever ready to sincerely acclaim every step the Stalinists take on the correct road . . . but sad to say, on November 1 Vaillant-Couturier takes a decisive step backward: the Fascists will be disarmed not by the united front but by the police of Doumergue, "under doctrine of "non-resistance to evil by violence," it should take for its symbol not the hammer and sickle, emblem of the October revolution, but the pious goat which provides Gandhi with his milk.

"But the arming of the workers is only opportune in a revolutionary situation, which does not yet exist." This profound argument means that the workers must permit themselves to be slaughtered until the situation becomes revolutionary. Those who yesterday preached the "third period" do not want to see what is going on before their eyes. The question of arms itself has only come forward because the "peaceful," "normal," "democratic" situation has given way to a stormy, critical and unstable situation which can transform itself into a revolutionary as well as a counter-revolutionary situation.

This alternative depends above all on whether the advanced workers will allow themselves to be attacked with impunity and defeated bit by bit or will reply to every blow by two of their own, arousing the courage of the oppressed and uniting them around their banner. A revolutionary situation does not fall from the skies. It takes form with the active participation of the revolutionary class and its party.

the pressure and control" of the united front. A remarkable idea: without revolution, by means of "ideological" pressure alone, to transform the Bonapartist police into an executive organ of the proletariat! Why then the armed conquest of power when the self-same results can be obtained in a peaceful way? "Under the pressure and control" of the united front Germain Martin nationalizes the banks, while Marchando will clap the reactionary plotters into prison, beginning with his colleague Tardieu. The idea of "pressure and control" in place of revolutionary struggle was not invented by Vaillant-Couturier. It was borrowed by him from Otto Bauer, Hilferding, and the Russian Menshevik Dan. The purpose of this idea is to divert the workers from revolutionary struggle. As a matter of fact, it is a hundred times easier to disarm the Fascists with one's own hands then with the hands of a hostile police. And when the united front will become sufficiently powerful to "control" the apparatus of the state—consequently after the seizure of power, and not before—it will simply drive away the bourgeois police and replace it with the workers' militia.—L.T.

The French Stalinists now argue that the militia did not safeguard the German proletariat from defeat. Only yesterday they completely denied any defeat in Germany and asserted that the policy of the German Stalinists was correct from beginning to end. Today they see the entire evil in the German workers' militia (Rote Front). Thus from one error they fall into a diametrically opposite one no less monstrous. The militia in itself does not settle the question. *A correct policy is necessary.* Meanwhile the policy of Stalinism in Germany ("social Fascism is the chief enemy," the split of the trade unions, the flirtation with nationalism, putschism) fatally led to the isolation of the proletarian vanguard and to its shipwreck. With an utterly worthless strategy no militia could have saved the situation.

It is nonsense to say that in itself the organization of the militia leads to adventures, provokes the enemy, replaces the political struggle by physical struggle, etc. In all these phrases there is nothing but political cowardice.

The militia, as the strong organization of the vanguard, is in fact the surest defense against adventures, against individual terrorism, against bloody spontaneous explosions.

The militia is at the same time the only serious way of reducing to a minimum the civil war which Fascism imposes upon the proletariat. Let the workers, despite the absence of a "revolutionary situation," occasionally correct the "papa's son" patriots in their own way and the recruitment of new Fascist bands will become incomparably more difficult.

But here the strategists, tangled in their own reasoning, bring forward against us still more stupefying arguments. We quote textually: "If we reply to the revolver shots of the Fascists with other revolver shots," writes *l'Humanité* of October 23 (1934) "we lose sight of the fact that Fascism is the product of the capitalist regime and that in fighting against Fascism it is the entire system which we face." It is difficult to accumulate in a few lines greater confusion or more errors. It is impossible to defend oneself against the Fascists because they are . . . "a product of the capitalist regime." That means we have to renounce the whole struggle, for all contemporary social evils are "products of the capitalist system."

When the Fascists kill a revolutionist or burn down the building of a proletarian newspaper, the workers are to sigh philosophically: "Alas! Murders and arson are products of the capitalist system," and go home with easy consciences. Fatalist prostration is substituted for the militant theory of Marx, to the sole advantage of the class enemy. The ruin of the petty bourgeoisie is, of course, the product of capitalism. The growth of the Fascist bands is, in turn, a product of the ruin of the petty bourgeoisie. But on the other hand, the increase in the misery and the revolt of the proletariat are also products of capitalism and the militia, in its turn, is the product of the sharpening of the class struggle. Why, then, for the "Marxists" of *l'Humanité* are the Fascist bands the legitimate product of capitalism and the workers' militia the illegitimate product of . . . the Trotskyists? It is impossible to make head or tail of this.

"We have to deal with the whole system," we are told. How? Over the heads of human beings? The Fascists in the different countries began with their revolvers and ended by destroying the whole "system" of workers' organizations. How else to check the armed offensive of the enemy if not by an armed defense in order, in our turn, to go over to the offensive?

L'Humanité now admits defense in words, but only in the form of "mass self-defense." The militia is harmful because, you see, it divides the combat detachments from the masses. But why then are there independent armed detachments among the Fascists who are not cut off from the reactionary masses but who, on the contrary, arouse the courage and embolden the masses by their well-organized attacks? Or perhaps the proletarian mass is inferior in combative quality to the declassed petty bourgeoisie?

Hopelessly tangled, *l'Humanité* finally begins to hesitate:

it appears that mass self-defense requires the creation of special "self-defense groups." In the place of the rejected militia special groups or detachments are proposed. It would seem at first sight that there is a difference only in the name. Certainly the name proposed by *l'Humanité* means nothing. One can speak of "mass self-defense" but it is impossible to speak of "self-defense groups" since the purpose of the groups is not to defend themselves but the workers' organizations. However, it is of course not a question of the name. The "self-defense groups," according to *l'Humanité*, must renounce the use of arms in order not to fall into "putschism." These sages treat the working class like an infant who must not be allowed to hold a razor in his hands. Razors, moreover, are the monopoly, as we know, of the Camelots du Roi, who are a legitimate "product of capitalism" and who with the aid of razors have overthrown the "system" of democracy. In any case, how are the "self-defense groups" going to defend themselves against the Fascist revolvers? "Ideologically," of course. In other words: they can only hide themselves. Not having what they require in their hands, they will have to seek "self-defense" in their feet. And the Fascists will in the meanwhile sack the workers' organizations with impunity. But if the proletariat suffers a terrible defeat, it will at any rate not have been guilty of "putschism." This fraudulent chatter, parading under the banner of "Bolshevism" arouses only disgust and loathing.

During the "third period" of happy memory, when the strategists of *l'Humanité* were afflicted with barricade delirium, "conquered" the streets every day and stamped as "social Fascist" everyone who did not share their extravagances, we predicted: "The moment these gentlemen burn the tips of their fingers, they will become the worst opportunists." That prediction has now been completely confirmed. At a time when within the Socialist Party the movement in favor of the militia is growing and strengthening, the leaders of the so-called Communist Party run for the hose to cool down the desire of the advanced workers to organize themselves in fighting columns. Could one imagine a more demoralizing or more damning work than this?

10. A Workers' Militia Must Be Built

In the ranks of the Socialist Party sometimes this objection is heard: "A militia must be formed but there is no need of shouting about it." One can only congratulate comrades who wish to protect the practical side of the business from inquisitive eyes and ears. But it would be much too naive to think that a militia could be created unseen and secretly within four walls. We need tens and later hundreds of thousands of fighters. They will come only if millions of men and women workers, and behind them the peasants, understand the necessity for the militia and create around the volunteers an atmosphere of ardent sympathy and active support. Conspiratorial care can and must envelop only the *technical* aspect of the matter. The *political* campaign must be openly developed, in meetings, factories, in the streets and on the public squares.

The fundamental cadres of the militia must be the factory workers grouped according to their place of work, known to each other and able to protect their combat detachments against the provocations of enemy agents far more easily and more surely than the most elevated bureaucrats. Conspirative general staffs without an open mobilization of the masses will at the moment of danger remain impotently suspended in mid-air. Every working class organization has to plunge into the job. In this question there can be no line of demarcation between the working class parties and the trade unions. Hand in hand they must mobilize the masses. The success of the people's militia will then be fully assured.

"But where are the workers going to get arms?" object the sober "realists,"—that is to say, frightened philistines—

31

"the enemy has rifles, cannon, tanks, gas and airplanes. The workers have a few hundred revolvers and pocket knives."

In this objection everything is piled up to frighten the workers. On the one hand, our sages identify the arms of the Fascists with the armament of the State. On the other, they turn towards the State and demand that it disarm the Fascists. Remarkable logic! In fact their position is false in both cases. In France the Fascists are still far from controlling the State. On February 6 they entered into armed conflict with the State police. That is why it is false to speak of cannon and tanks when it is a matter of the *immediate* armed struggle against the Fascists. The Fascists, of course, are richer than we. It is easier for them to buy arms. But the workers are more numerous, more determined, more devoted, when they are conscious of a firm revolutionary leadership.

In addition to other sources, the workers can arm themselves at the expense of the Fascists by systematically disarming them.

This is now one of the most serious forms of the struggle against Fascism. When workers' arsenals will begin to stock up at the expense of the Fascist arms depots, the banks and trusts will be more prudent in financing the armament of their murderous guards. It would even be possible in this case—*but in this case only*—that the alarmed authorities would really begin to prevent the arming of the Fascists in order not to provide an additional source of arms for the workers. We have known for a long time that only a revolutionary tactic engenders, as a by-product, "reforms" or concessions from the government.

But how to disarm the Fascists? Naturally, it is impossible to do so with newspaper articles alone. Fighting squads must be created. An intelligence service must be established. Thousands of informers and friendly helpers will volunteer from all sides when they realize that the business has been seriously undertaken by us. It requires a will to proletarian action.

But the arms of the Fascists are of course not the only source. In France there are more than one million organized workers. Generally speaking, this number is small. But it is entirely sufficient to make a beginning in the organization of a workers' militia. If the parties and unions armed only a tenth of their members, that would already be a force of 100,000 men. There is no doubt whatever that the number of volunteers who would come forward on the morrow of a "united front" appeal for a workers' militia would far exceed that number. The contributions of the parties and unions, collections and voluntary subscriptions would within a month or two make it possible to assure the arming of 100,000 to 200,000 working class fighters. The Fascist rabble would immediately sink its tail between its legs. The whole perspective of development would become incomparably more favorable.

To invoke the absence of arms or other objective reasons to explain why no attempt has been made up to now to create a militia, is to fool oneself and others. The principle obstacle—one can say the only obstacle—has its roots in the conservative and passive character of the leaders of the workers' organizations. The skeptics who are the leaders do not believe in the strength of the proletariat. They put their hope in all sorts of miracles from above instead of giving a revolutionary outlet to the energies pulsing below. The socialist workers must compel their leaders to pass over immediately to the creation of the workers' militia or else give way to younger, fresher forces.

11. The Arming of the Proletariat

A strike is inconceivable without propaganda and without agitation. It is also inconceivable without pickets who, when they can, use persuasion, but when obliged, use force. The strike is the most elementary form of the class struggle which always combines, in varying proportions, "ideological" methods with physical methods. The struggle against

LEON TROTSKY

Fascism is basically a political struggle which needs a militia just as the strike needs pickets. Basically, the picket is the embryo of the workers' militia. He who thinks of renouncing "physical" struggle must renounce all struggle, for the spirit does not live without flesh.

Following the splendid phrase of the great military theoretician, Clausewitz, war is the continuation of politics by other means. This definition also fully applies to civil war. Physical struggle is only "another means" of the political struggle. It is impermissible to oppose one to the other since it is impossible to check at will the political struggle when it transforms itself, by force of inner necessity, into a physical struggle.

The duty of a revolutionary party is to foresee in time the inescapability of the transformation of politics into open armed conflict, and with all its forces to prepare for that moment just as the ruling classes are preparing.

The militia detachments for defense against Fascism are the first step on the road to the arming of the proletariat, not the last. Our slogan is:

Arm the proletariat and the revolutionary peasants.

The workers' militia must in the final analysis embrace all the toilers. To fulfill this program *completely* would be possible only in a workers' State into whose hands would pass all the means of production and consequently also all the means of destruction, i.e., all the arms and the factories which produce them.

However, it is impossible to arrive at a workers' State with empty hands. Only political invalids like Renaudel can speak of a peaceful, constitutional road to socialism. The constitutional road is cut by trenches held by the Fascist bands. There are not a few trenches before us. The bourgeoisie will not hesitate to resort to a dozen *coups d'état* aided by the police and the army, to prevent the proletariat from coming to power.

A workers' socialist State can be created only by a victorious revolution.

34

WHITHER FRANCE?

Every revolution is prepared by the march of economic and political development, but it is always decided by open armed conflicts between hostile classes. A revolutionary victory can become possible only as a result of long political agitation, a lengthy period of education and organization of the masses.

But the armed conflict itself must likewise be prepared long in advance.

The advanced workers must know that they will have to fight and win a death struggle. They must reach out for arms, as a guarantee of their emancipation.

In an era as critical as the present, the party of the revolution must unceasingly preach to the workers the need for arming themselves and must do everything to assure the arming, at least, of the proletarian vanguard. Without this, victory is impossible.

The most recent electoral victories of the British Labor Party do not at all invalidate what is said above. Even if we were to allow that the next parliamentary elections will give the Labor Party an absolute majority, which is not assured in any case; if we were further to allow that the party would actually take the road of socialist transformations—which is scarcely probable—it would immediately meet with such fierce resistance from the House of Lords, the king, the banks, the stock-market, the bureaucracy, the press, that a split in its ranks would become inevitable, and the Left, more radical wing would become a parliamentary minority. Simultaneously the Fascist movement would acquire an unprecedented sweep. Alarmed by the municipal elections, the British bourgeoisie is no doubt already actively preparing for an extra-parliamentary struggle while the tops of the Labor Party lull the proletariat with the successes and are compelled, unfortunately, to see the British events through the rosy spectacles of Jean Longuet. In point of fact, the less the leaders of the Labor Party prepare for it, the more cruel will be the civil war forced upon the proletariat by the British bourgeoisie.

"But where will you get arms for the whole proletariat?" object once more the skeptics who mistake their own inner futility for an objective impossibility. They forget that the same question has been posed before every revolution in history. And despite everything, victorious revolutions mark important stages in the development of humanity.

The proletariat produces arms, transports them, erects the buildings in which they are kept, defends these buildings against itself, serves in the army and creates all its equipment. It is neither locks nor walls which separate the proletariat from arms, but the habit of submission, the hypnosis of class domination and nationalist poison.

It is sufficient to destroy these psychological walls—and no wall of stone will stand in the way. It is enough that the proletariat should want arms—and it will find them. The task of the revolutionary party is to awaken this desire and to facilitate its realization.

But here Frossard and hundreds of frightened parliamentarians, journalists and trade union officials, advance their last argument, the weightiest: "Can serious men in general place their hopes in the success of physical struggle after the recent tragic experiences in Austria and Spain? Think of present day technique, tanks, gas, airplanes!!" This argument only shows that a number of "serious men" not only want to learn nothing but in their fear even forget what little they ever learned.

The history of the last 20 years demonstrates with particular clarity that the fundamental problems in the relations among classes, as among nations, are settled by physical force. The pacifists have long hoped that the growth of military technique would make war impossible. The philistines have repeated for decades that the growth of military technique would make revolution impossible. However, wars and revolutions continue. Never have there been so many revolutions, including victorious revolutions, as there have been since the last war which uncovered all the might of military technique.

Frossard and Co. offer old clichés as though they were the latest discoveries, invoking instead of automatic rifles and machine guns, tanks and bombing planes. We reply: behind each machine there are men who are linked not only by technical but by social and political bonds. When historic development poses before society an unpostponable revolutionary task as a question of life or death, when there exists a progressive class with whose victory is joined the salvation of society—then the development itself of the political struggle opens up before the revolutionary class the most varied possibilities—as much to paralyze the military force of the enemy as to win it over, at least partially. In the mind of a philistine these possibilities always appear as "lucky accidents" which will never be repeated. In fact, in the most unexpected but fundamentally natural combinations, possibilities of every sort open up in every great, i. e., truly popular, revolution. But despite everything victory does not come of itself.

To utilize the favorable possibilities it is necessary to have a revolutionary will, an iron determination to conquer, a bold and perspicacious leadership. *L'Humanité* agrees in words with the slogan of "arming the workers" but only to renounce it in deeds. At the present time, according to this paper, it is inadmissible to advance a slogan which is only opportune "in a full revolutionary crisis." It is dangerous to load your rifle, says the "too-prudent" hunter so long as the game remains invisible. But when the game puts in an appearance it is a little too late to load the rifle. Do the strategists of *l'Humanité* really think that in "the full revolutionary crisis" they will be able without any preparation to mobilize and arm the proletariat? To secure a large quantity of arms, one needs a certain quantity on hand. One needs military cadres. One needs the invincible desire of the masses to secure arms. One needs uninterrupted preparatory work not only in the gymnasiums but in indissoluble connection with the daily struggle of the masses. This means:

It is necessary immediately to build the militia and at the same time to carry on propaganda for the general armament of the revolutionary workers and peasants.

12. BUT THE DEFEATS IN AUSTRIA AND SPAIN . . .

The impotence of parliamentarianism in the conditions of the crisis of the whole capitalist system is so obvious that the vulgar democrats in the camp of the workers (Renaudel, Frossard and their imitators) do not find a single argument to defend their petrified prejudices. All the more readily do they seize upon every defeat and every failure suffered along the revolutionary road. The development of their thought is this: if pure parliamentarianism offers no way out, armed struggle does no better. The defeats of the proletarian insurrections in Austria and in Spain are now, of course, their choice argument. In fact, in their criticism of the revolutionary method the theoretical and political bankruptcy of the vulgar democrats appears still more clearly than in their defense of the methods of rotting bourgeois democracy.

No one has said that the revolutionary method automatically assures victory. What is decisive is not the method in itself but its correct application, the Marxist orientation in events, powerful organization, the confidence of the masses won through long experience, a perspicacious and bold leadership. The issue of every struggle depends upon the moment and conditions of the conflict and the relation of forces. Marxism is quite far from the thought that armed conflict is the only revolutionary method, or a panacea good under all conditions. Marxism in general knows no fetishes, neither parliamentary nor insurrectional. There is a time and place for everything. There is one thing that one can say at the beginning:

On the parliamentary road the socialist proletariat nowhere and never conquered power nor ever even as yet has drawn close to it.

WHITHER FRANCE?

The governments of Scheidemann, Hermann Müller, Mac-Donald, had nothing in common with socialism. The bourgeoisie permitted the social democrats and Laborites to come to power only on condition that they defend capitalism against its enemies. They scrupulously fulfilled this condition. Purely parliamentary, anti-revolutionary socialism nowhere and never resulted in a socialist ministry. It did succeed in producing loathsome renegades who exploited the workers' party to carve out cabinet careers—Millerand, Briand, Viviani, Laval, Paul-Boncour, Marquet.

On the other hand, historical experience shows that the revolutionary method can lead to the conquest of power by the proletariat—in Russia in 1917, in Germany and Austria in 1918, in Spain in 1930. In Russia there was a powerful Bolshevik party which prepared for the revolution over a long period of years and knew solidly how to take over power.

The reformist parties of Germany, Austria and Spain did not prepare the revolution, did not lead it, but suffered it.

Frightened by the power which had come into their hands against their own will, they benevolently handed it over to the bourgeoisie. In this way they undermined the confidence of the proletariat in itself and, further, the confidence of the petty bourgeoisie in the proletariat. They prepared the conditions for the growth of Fascist reaction and fell victims to it.

Civil war, we have said, following Clausewitz, is a continuation of politics but by other means. This means that the result of the civil war depends for one-fourth, not to say one-tenth, upon the development of the civil war itself, its technical means, its purely military leadership, and for three-fourths, if not for nine-tenths, on the political preparation. Of what does this political preparation consist? It is in the revolutionary cohesion of the masses, in their liberation from servile hopes in the clemency, generosity and loyalty of "democratic slave-owners," in the education of revolutionary cadres who know how to defy official public opinion and who know how to display towards the bourgeoisie one-tenth the implacability which the bourgeoisie displays towards the toilers. Without this temper, civil war when conditions force it—*and they always end by forcing it*—will take place under conditions most unfavorable for the proletariat, will depend upon many hazards and then, even in case of military victory, power can escape the hands of the proletariat. Whoever does not foresee that the class struggle leads inevitably to armed conflict is blind. But he is no less blind who fails to see behind this armed conflict and its outcome the whole previous policy of the classes in struggle.

What was defeated in Austria was not the method of insurrection but Austro-Marxism and in Spain unprincipled parliamentary reformism.

In 1918, the Austrian Social Democracy handed over to the bourgeoisie, behind the back of the proletariat, the power which the latter had won. In 1927, it not only turned away in cowardly fashion from the proletarian insurrection which had every chance of victory, but led the workers' Schutzbund against the insurgent masses. Thus it prepared the victory of Dollfuss. Bauer and Co. said: "We desire peaceful evolution but if the enemy loses his head and attacks us, then. . . ."

This formula appeared very "wise" and very "realistic." Unfortunately, it is on this Austro-Marxist model that Marceau Pivert also constructs his reasoning: "If—then." In fact, this formula is a snare for the workers. It lulls them and deceives them. "If" means that the forms of the struggle depend upon the good-will of the bourgeoisie and not upon the absolute irreconcilability of class interests. "If" means that *if* we are wise, prudent, conciliatory, the bourgeoisie will be loyal and everything will proceed peacefully.

Running after the phantom "if," Otto Bauer and the other leaders of the Austrian Social Democracy passively retreated before the reaction, ceded one position after another, demoralized the masses, retreated again, until they found themselves in the final impasse. There on the last redoubt they accepted battle and lost it.

In Spain events took a different course but the causes of the defeat were basically the same. The Socialist Party, like the Russian Social Revolutionaries and Mensheviks, shared power with the republican bourgeoisie to prevent the workers and peasants from carrying the revolution to its conclusion. For two years the Socialists in power helped the bourgeoisie disembarrass itself of the masses by crumbs of national, social and agrarian reforms. Against the most revolutionary strata of the people, the Socialists used repression.

The result was twofold. Anarcho-syndicalism, which would have melted like wax in the heat of revolution had the workers' party pursued a correct course, was strengthened and drew around it the militant layers of the proletariat. At the other pole, social catholic demagogy succeeded in skillfully exploiting the discontent of the masses with the bourgeois-socialist government.

When the Socialist Party was sufficiently compromised, the bourgeoisie drove it from power and took over the offensive on the whole front. The Socialist Party had to defend itself under the most unfavorable conditions which had been prepared for it by its own previous policy. The bourgeoisie already had a mass support at the Right. The anarcho-syndicalist leaders, who during the course of the revolution committed all the mistakes typical of these professional confusionists, refused to support the insurrection led by the traitor "politicians." The movement did not take on a general character but remained sporadic. The government directed its blows at the scattered sections of the workers. The civil war forced by the reaction ended in the defeat of the proletariat.

From the Spanish experience it is not difficult to draw conclusions against socialist participation in a bourgeois government. The conclusion itself is indisputable but utterly insufficient. The alleged "radicalism" of Austro-Marxism is in no sense any better than Spanish ministerialism. The difference between them is technical, not political. Both waited for the bourgeosie to give them "loyalty" for "loyalty." Both led the proletariat to catastrophe.

In Spain as in Austria it was not revolutionary methods which were defeated but opportunist methods in a revolutionary situation. It is not the same thing!

We shall not stop here on the policy of the Communist International in Austria and in Spain. We refer the reader to the files of *La Vérité* and a series of pamphlets of recent years.* In an exceptionally favorable situation the Austrian and Spanish Communist Parties, fettered by the theory of the "third period" and "social Fascism," etc., found themselves doomed to complete isolation. Compromising the methods of revolution by the authority of "Moscow" they barred, thereby, the road to a truly Marxist, truly Bolshevik policy. The fundamental faculty of revolution is to submit to a rapid and pitiless examination all doctrines and all methods. The punishment almost immediately follows the crime.

The responsibility of the Communist International for the defeats of the proletariat in Germany, Austria and in Spain is incommensurable. It is not sufficient to carry out a "revolutionary" policy (in words). A *correct* policy is needed. No one has yet found any other secret of victory.

* See files of the *Militant*, New York, 1929-34, *New Militant*, 1934-36, and the following works of Trotsky, issued by Pioneer Publishers:
The Turn in the Communist International and the German Situation (Communist League of America), 1930.
The Revolution in Spain, March, 1931.
The Spanish Revolution in Danger, June, 1931.
What Next? 1932.
The Only Road For Germany, 1933.
The Third International After Lenin, 1936.

13. The United Front and the Struggle for Power

We have already said that the united front of the Socialist and Communist Parties embodies immense possibilities.
If only it wants it seriously, it will tomorrow become master
in France. But the will must be there.

The fact that Jouhaux and, in general, the bureaucracy
of the C.G.T.* remain *outside* the united front preserving
their "independence" seems to contradict what we say. But
that is only at first sight. In an epoch of great tasks and
great dangers which bring the masses to their feet, the bar-
riers between the political and trade union organizations of
the proletariat disappear. The workers want to know how
to save themselves from unemployment and Fascism, how to
win independence from capital, and they are scarcely concerned with the "independence" of Jouhaux from proletarian policy (on bourgeois policy Jouhaux is, alas, quite
dependent). If the proletarian vanguard represented in the
united front correctly treads the path of struggle, all the
obstacles established by the trade union bureaucracy will be
overthrown by the living torrent of the proletariat. The
key to the situation is now in the united front. If it does
not use this key it will play the lamentable role which would
inevitably have been played by the united front of the Mensheviks and Social Revolutionaries in Russia in 1917, if . . .
if the Bolsheviks had not prevented them from doing so.

We shall not speak of the Socialist and Communist Parties in particular because both have renounced their independence in favor of the united front. As soon as the two
working class parties which sharply competed in the past
renounced mutual criticism and the winning of adherents
from each other, by that alone they ceased to exist as dis-
tinct parties. To invoke "principled differences" which remain, changes nothing. As soon as principled differences are
not manifested openly and actively, at a moment as laden

* General Confederation of Labor.

with responsibility as the present, they cease thereby to exist politically. They are like treasure which rests on the bottom of the ocean. We do not predict whether the common work will end in fusion but for the present period, which is of decisive importance for the destiny of France, the united front operates like an incomplete party constructed on the federalist principle.

What does the united front want? Until now it has not told the masses. The struggle against Fascism? But until now the united front has not explained *how* it proposes to fight against Fascism. Besides, a purely defensive bloc against Fascism could only suffice if in everything else the two parties preserved complete independence. But no, we have a united front which embraces almost the entire public activity of the two parties and excludes their reciprocal struggle to win the majority of the proletariat. From this situation all the consequences must be drawn. The first and the most important is the struggle for power. The aim of the united front can be only a government of the united front, i.e., a Socialist-Communist government, a Blum-Cachin ministry.

This must be said openly. If the united front takes itself seriously—and it is only on this condition that the popular masses will take it seriously—it cannot divest itself of the slogan of conquest of power. By what means? By every means which leads to that end.

The united front does not renounce parliamentary struggle but it utilizes parliament above all to unmask its impotence and to explain to the people that the present government has an extra-parliamentary base and that it can be overthrown only by a powerful mass movement.

The struggle for power means the utilization of all the possibilities provided by the semi-parliamentary Bonapartist regime to overthrow this regime by a revolutionary push, to replace the bourgeois state by a workers' state.

The last district elections showed an increase in the Socialist and especially the Communist vote. In itself this fact settles nothing. The German Communist Party on the eve of its collapse had an incomparably more striking increase of votes. New, broad strata of the oppressed are driven to the Left by the whole situation, independently even of the policy of the extreme parties. The French Communist Party gained more votes because by tradition it remains, despite its present conservative policy, the "extreme Left." The masses showed by this their tendency to give the working class parties an impulsion *to the Left,* for the masses are infinitely more to the Left than their parties. Further testimony of this is the revolutionary spirit of the Socialist youth. It must not be forgotten that the youth is the sensitive barometer of the whole class and its vanguard!

If the united front does not emerge from passivity or, worse still, if it enters upon an unworthy romance with the Radicals, then to the "Left" of the united front Anarchists, Anarcho-Syndicalists and other similar groupings of political disintegration will be strengthened. At the same time apathy, precursor of catastrophe, will make headway.

On the other hand, the united front assuring its rear and its flanks against the Fascist bands opens up a *broad political offensive under the slogan of conquest of power.* It will awaken an echo so powerful as to exceed the most optimistic expectations.

Only hollow charlatans for whom great mass movements shall always remain a book sealed with seven seals can fail to understand this.

14. NOT A PROGRAM OF PASSIVITY BUT A PROGRAM OF REVOLUTION

The struggle for power must begin with the fundamental idea that if opposition to further aggravation of the situation of the masses under capitalism is still possible, no real improvement of their situation is conceivable without a revolutionary invasion of the right of capitalist property. The political campaign of the united front must base itself upon

LEON TROTSKY

a well elaborated *transition program,* i. e., on a system of measures which with a workers' and peasants' government can assure the transition from capitalism to socialism.

Now a program is needed not to ease the conscience but to guide revolutionary action. What is a program worth if it remains a dead letter? The Belgian Workers' Party, for example, adopted the pompous plan of De Man with all its "nationalizations." But what sense was there in it when the party did not lift its little finger to realize it? Programs of Fascism are fantastic, false, demagogic. But Fascism carries on a fierce struggle for power. Socialism can advance the most scientific program but its value will be equal to zero if the vanguard of the proletariat does not unfold a bold struggle to capture the state. The social crisis in its political expression is the crisis of power. The old master of society is bankrupt. A new master is needed.

If the revolutionary proletariat does not take power, Fascism will inevitably take it!

A program of transitional demands for "the middle classes" can naturally assume great importance if this program corresponds, on the one hand, to the real needs of the middle classes, and on the other, to the demands of the development towards socialism.* But once more the center of gravity does not exist now in a special program. The middle classes have seen many programs. What they need is confidence that the program will be realized. The moment the peasant says: "This time it seems that the working class parties will not retreat"—the cause of socialism is won.

* In *l'Ecole Emancipée* comrade J. Serret published an interesting questionnaire describing the economic situation of various strata of the peasantry and their political tendencies. The public school teachers could become irreplaceable agents of the united front in the village and play an historic role in the coming period but to do so they must come out of their shell. The time is truly unfavorable for small experiments and small laboratories. The revolutionary teachers must enter the Socialist Party to strengthen its revolutionary wing and link it up with the peasant masses. Waste of time is criminal.—L.T.

46

But for that it is necessary to show in action that we are firmly prepared to smash every obstacle in our path.

There is no need of inventing means of struggle. They are provided by the whole history of the world working class movement.

A concentrated campaign in the working class press pounding steadily on the same key; real socialist speeches from the tribune of parliament, not by tame deputies but by leaders of the people; the utilization of every electoral campaign for revolutionary purposes; repeated meetings to which the masses come not merely to hear the speakers but to get the slogans and directives of the hour; the creation and strengthening of the workers' militia; well organized demonstrations driving the reactionary bands from the streets; protest strikes; an open campaign for the unification and enlargement of the trade union ranks under the banner of resolute class struggle; stubborn, carefully calculated activity to win the army over to the cause of the people; broader strikes; more powerful demonstrations; the general strike of toilers of town and country; a general offensive against the Bonapartist government for the workers' and peasants' power.

There is still time to prepare for victory. Fascism has not yet become a mass movement. The inevitable decomposition of Radicalism will mean, however, the narrowing of the base of Bonapartism, the growth of the two extreme camps and the approach of the showdown. It is not a question of years but of months. The length of this period is not fixed by anyone but depends upon the struggle of living forces and above all upon the policy of the proletariat and its united front.

The potential forces of the revolution exceed by far the forces of Fascism and in general of the whole united reaction. Skeptics who think that all is lost must be pitilessly driven out of the workers' ranks. From the depths of the masses come vibrant echoes to every bold word, every truly revolutionary slogan. The masses want the struggle.

LEON TROTSKY

It is not the spirit of combination among parliamentarians and journalists, but the legitimate and creative hatred of the oppressed for the oppressors which is today the single most progressive factor in history. It is necessary to turn to the masses, toward their deepest layers. It is necessary to appeal to their passions and to their reason. It is necessary to reject the false "prudence" which is a synonym for cowardice and which, at great historical turning points, amounts to treason. The united front must take for its motto the formula of Danton: *"De l'audace, toujours de l'audace, et encore de l'audace."** To understand the situation fully and to draw from it all the practical conclusions, boldly and without fear and to the end, is to assure the victory of Socialism.

November 9, 1934

---

* "Audacity, always audacity, and still more audacity."

2

Once Again, Whither France?

THE FRENCH PEOPLE have arrived at the crossroads: one way leads to the socialist revolution; the other to Fascist catastrophe. The choice depends on the working class. At its head is the organized vanguard. Again we put the question: "Where will the proletarian vanguard lead France?"

In January, the C.E.C. of the Socialist Party launched a program of *struggle for power, the destruction of the mechanism of the bourgeois state, the setting up of the workers' and peasants' democracy, the expropriation of banks and heavy industry.* However, up to the present, the party has not made the slightest attempt to bring this program before the masses. The Communist Party, in turn, has absolutely refused to come out for the struggle for power. The reason? "The situation is not revolutionary."

The workers' militia? The arming of the workers? Workers' control? A plan of nationalization? Impossible. "The situation is not revolutionary." What, then, can we do? Launch weighty petitions with the clergy, compete in empty eloquence with the Radical Socialists and wait? Wait how long? Until the situation becomes revolutionary of its own accord. The scholarly doctors of the Communist International have a thermometer which they place under the tongue of old lady History, and by this means they infallibly determine the revolutionary temperature. But they don't show anyone their thermometer.

We submit: the diagnosis of the Comintern is entirely

false. The situation is revolutionary, as revolutionary as it can be, *granted the non-revolutionary policies of the working class parties.* More exactly, the situation is pre-revolutionary. In order to bring the situation to its full maturity, there must be an immediate, vigorous, unremitting mobilization of the masses, under the slogan of the conquest of power in the name of socialism. This is the only way through which the pre-revolutionary situation will be changed into a revolutionary situation. On the other hand, if we continue to mark time, the pre-revolutionary situation will inevitably be changed into one of counter-revolution, and will bring on the victory of Fascism.

At the present time, all that the pious mouthings of the phrase "non-revolutionary situation" can do is to crush the minds of the workers, paralyze their will and hand them over to the class enemy. Under the cover of such phrases, conservatism, indolence, stupidity and cowardice take possession of the leadership of the proletariat, and the ground is laid, as it was in Germany, for catastrophe.

In the pages which follow, we, the Bolshevik-Leninists, will submit the analyses and predictions of the Communist International to a detailed, Marxist criticism. At times we will touch on the points of view of various Socialist leaders, to the extent that this is needed for our fundamental purpose: namely, to show the radical falsity of the policies of the Central Committee of the French Communist Party. To the shouts and insults of the Stalinists we oppose facts and arguments.

We shall not, of course, stop with a merely negative criticism. To the false points of view and false slogans we shall oppose the creative ideas and methods of Marx and Lenin.

We ask the reader to pay close attention. We are concerned here in the most immediate and literal sense with the lives of the French workers. No class conscious worker has the right to be passive in the face of these problems, upon the solution of which depends the fate of his class.

ONCE AGAIN, WHITHER FRANCE?

1. How a Revolutionary Situation Arises

The first and most important premise of a revolutionary situation is the most intense sharpening of the contradictions between the productive forces and the property relations. *The nation stops going forward.* . The arrest in the economic development and, even more, its regression signify that the capitalist system of production is definitely worn out and must give way to the socialist system.

The present crisis, which encompasses all countries and thrusts economy back decades, has definitely pushed the bourgeois system to absurdity. If, at the dawn of capitalism, ignorant and starving workers broke machines, today it is the capitalists themselves who destroy machines and factories. The further maintenance of the private ownership of the means of production threatens humanity with degeneration and barbarism.

The basis of society is economic. That basis is ripe for socialism in a double sense: modern technology has advanced to a point where it can assure a high standard of living to the nation and to all mankind; but the capitalist property system, which has outlived itself, dooms the masses to ever-increasing poverty and suffering.

The fundamental premise of socialism—that is, the economic premise—has already been present for some time. But capitalism will not disappear from the scene *automatically.* Only the working class can seize the forces of production from the stranglehold of the exploiters. History places this task squarely before us. If the proletariat is, for one reason or another, incapable of routing the bourgeoisie and of seizing power, if it is, for example, paralyzed by its own parties and trade unions, the continued decay of economy and civilization will follow, calamities will pile up, despair and prostration will engulf the masses, and capitalism—decrepit, decayed, rotting—will strangle the people with in-

51

creasing strength, and will thrust them into the abyss of a new war.

Other than the socialist revolution, there is no way out.

At first the Presidium of the Comintern tried to explain that the crisis which started in 1929 was the last crisis of capitalism. Two years afterward, Stalin declared that the present crisis, "truly understood," was not yet the last. We also meet the same attempt at prophecy in the socialist camp: "Is it the final crisis, or is it not?"

"It is imprudent to say," wrote Blum in *Populaire*, February 23, "that the present crisis is the final spasm of capitalism, the last death throe before agony and decay." Grumbach had the same point of view when he said at Mulhouse on February 26: "Some say this crisis is a passing phase, others see it as the final crisis of capitalism. We do not yet dare to take a definite position."

In this manner of putting the question there are two cardinal errors: first, it confuses the *cyclical crisis* with the *historical crisis of the whole capitalist system;* second, it assumes that independently of the conscious activity of classes, a crisis can be *by itself* the "last" crisis.

Under the domination of industrial capital, in the era of free competition, the cyclical booms exceeded by far the crises: the first were the "rule," the second the "exception." Capitalism in its entirety was advancing. Since the war, with the domination of monopoly finance-capital, the cyclical crises far exceed the upswings. We may say that the crises have become the "rule" and the booms the "exceptions"; economic development in its entirety has been going down and not up.

However, the cyclical oscillations are inevitable, and, with capitalism in decline, they will continue as long as capitalism exists. And capitalism will continue until the proletarian revolution is achieved. This is the only correct answer to the question: "Is this the final crisis of capitalism?"

The revolutionary worker must, before all else, understand that Marxism, the only scientific theory of the proletarian revolution, has nothing in common with the fatalistic hope for the "final" crisis. Marxism is, in its very essence, a set of directives for revolutionary action. Marxism does not overlook will and courage, but rather aids them to find the right road.

There is no crisis which can be, by itself, fatal to capitalism. The oscillations of the business cycle only create a situation in which it will be easier, or more difficult, for the proletariat to overthrow capitalism. The transition from a bourgeois society to a socialist society presupposes the activity of living men who are the makers of their own history. They do not make history by accident, or according to their caprice, but under the influence of objectively determined causes. However, their own actions—their initiative, audacity, devotion, and likewise their stupidity and cowardice—are necessary links in the chain of historical development.

The crises of capitalism are not numbered, nor is it indicated in advance which one of these will be the "last." But our entire epoch and, above all, the present crisis imperiously command the proletariat: "Seize Power!" If, however, the party of the working class, in spite of favorable conditions, reveals itself incapable of leading the proletariat to the seizure of power, the life of society will continue necessarily upon capitalist foundations—until a new crisis, a new war, perhaps until the complete disintegration of European civilization.

The imperialist war of 1914-1918 was also a "crisis" in the career of capitalism, and, indeed, the most terrible of all possible crises. No book carried the prediction whether the war would be the last *bloody* folly of capitalism. The experience of Russia showed that the war *might* have been the end of capitalism. In Germany and Austria, the fate of bourgeois society in 1918 depended entirely upon the Social Democracy, but the Social Democracy revealed itself as the handmaiden of capitalism. In Italy and France, the proletariat might have seized power at the end of the war, but it did not have a revolutionary party at its head. In a

word, if the Second International had not, at the time of
the war, betrayed the cause of socialism to bourgeois patriotism, the whole history of Europe and of mankind might
today be entirely different. Assuredly, the past is irrevoc-
able. But one can, and one ought, to learn the lessons of the
past.

The development of Fascism is, in itself, irrefutable wit-
ness to the fact that the working class has been tragically
late in fulfilling the task imposed upon it a long time ago by
the decline of capitalism.

The phrase "this is not yet the 'last' crisis" can have only
one meaning: in spite of the lessons of the war and the convulsions of the post-war period, the working class parties
are not yet able to prepare either themselves or the proletariat for the seizure of power; still worse, the leaders of
these parties do not yet understand the task confronting
them—they reject it for themselves, their party and their
class, and hand it over to "the process of historical development." Their fatalism is a betrayal of the theory of
Marxism, and a justification for a political betrayal of the
proletariat, that is, the preparation for a new capitulation
to a new "last" war.

* * *

The fatalism of the Social Democracy is a heritage of the
pre-war period, when capitalism was advancing almost without interruption, when the number of workers was increasing,
and when the number of party members, votes at elections
and parliamentary representatives was growing. From
this automatic rise was born little by little the reformist illusion that it was enough to continue along the old road
(propaganda, elections, organization) and victory would
come of itself.

The war, no doubt, interfered with this automatic development. But the war was an "exceptional" phenomenon.
With the help of Geneva there would be no new war, everything would return to normal and the automatic development would be re-established.

In the light of this perspective, the words "This is not yet the 'last' crisis" meant: "In five years, in ten years or in twenty years, we will have more votes, more representatives, and then, let us hope, we shall take power." (See the articles and lectures of Paul Faure.) This optimistic fatalism, which seemed convincing for a quarter of a century, today resounds like a voice from the grave. It is a radically false idea that in going towards the future crisis the proletariat will inevitably become more powerful than at present. With the further inevitable decay of capitalism, the proletariat will not grow and reinforce itself but will decompose, constantly increasing the army of the unemployed and slum-proletariat. The petty bourgeoisie, meanwhile, will be declassed and sink into despair. Loss of time holds out the perspective of Fascism, and not of proletarian revolution.

It is worth remarking that the Comintern, bureaucratized to the marrow, has replaced the theory of revolutionary action with a religion of fatalism. It is impossible to fight because there is no "revolutionary situation." But a revolutionary situation does not fall from the sky. It comes about in the class struggle. The party of the working class is the most important *political* factor in the development of a revolutionary situation. If this party turns its back on its revolutionary task, lulling the workers to sleep and deceiving them into playing with petitions and fraternizing with Radical Socialists, the situation that comes about will be not revolutionary, but counter-revolutionary.

The *decline of capitalism*, together with the extraordinarily high level of the productive forces, is the economic premise of the socialist revolution. On this foundation the *class struggle* takes place. A *revolutionary situation* develops and matures in the living struggle of the classes.

How does the big bourgeoisie, master of modern society, size up the present situation? And what is it doing? The 6th of February, 1934, was unexpected only by the organizations of the working class and the petty bourgeoisie. The leading bodies of finance-capital prepared the plot over a

long period of time, intending, by violence, to substitute
Bonapartism ("personal" rule) for parliamentarianism.
That is to say, the banks, the trusts, the General Staff, the
capitalist press believed the danger of revolution to be so
close, so immediate, that they hastened to prepare for it by
a "little" *coup d'état.*

Two important conclusions follow from this fact: 1) the
capitalists, at the beginning of 1934, believed the situation
to be revolutionary; 2) they were not content to await passively the development of events, to resort to "legalistic"
defense at the last minute, but they took the initiative themselves by sending their gangs into the streets. The big bourgeoisie taught the workers an inestimable lesson in the
strategy of class warfare.

L'Humanité maintains that the "United Front" drove
Doumergue out of office. But that is hollow bombast, to say
the least. On the contrary, if finance-capital believed it possible and feasible to replace Doumergue by Flandin, it is
precisely because the United Front, as experience proved to
the bourgeoisie, does not yet represent an immediate revolutionary danger. "Since the formidable leaders of the Comintern, in spite of the situation in France, did not prepare
for struggle, but trembled with fear, that means that we
can wait a while before making use of Fascism. It is useless
to force events and compromise the Radical Socialists prematurely, since we may still have need of them." This is
what the true masters of the situation said. They upheld
the Cabinet of the National Union and its Bonapartist decrees, they terrorized parliament, but they allowed Doumergue to go back to sleep. Thus the leaders of the
bourgeoisie introduced a certain correction into their first
analysis, recognizing that the situation was not so much
immediately revolutionary as pre-revolutionary.

A second remarkable lesson in class strategy! It shows
that even finance-capital, with the levers of the whole social
machine under its control, cannot infallibly estimate, at a
single *a priori* glance, the full reality of a political situa-

tion. It enters into the struggle and, in the development of
the struggle, on basis of experience gained in the struggle, it corrects its analysis and makes it more precise. This,
in general, is the only possible method in political questions
of being oriented correctly and at the same time actively.

And the leaders of the Communist International? In
Moscow, away from the French working class, a few badly
informed, mediocre bureaucrats—the majority of them even
unable to read French—pronounced an infallible diagnosis,
with the aid of their thermometer: "The situation is not
revolutionary." The Central Committee of the French Communist Party is obliged to close its eyes and ears and repeat this hollow phrase. The road of the Communist International is the shortest road to the abyss!

*   *   *

The Radical Socialist Party represents that political instrument of the big bourgeoisie which is the best adapted to
the traditions and prejudices of the petty bourgeoisie. In
spite of this, the most responsible leaders of Radical Socialism, under the whip of finance-capital, bowed humbly before
the *coup d'etat* of February 6, though it was directed in
the first instance against them. For they recognized that
the development of the class struggle threatened the fundamental interests of the "nation," that is to say, of the bourgeoisie, and they felt obliged to sacrifice the parliamentary
interests of their party. The capitulation of the most powerful parliamentary party before the guns and knives of the
Fascists is an external expression of the complete upset in
the political equilibrium of the country. But to say this—
is to say that the situation is revolutionary, or, more exactly, pre-revolutionary.*

* It is extremely characteristic of the frightened, petty bourgeois
working class bureaucracy, especially the Stalinists, that it entered
into an alliance with the Radical-Socialists to "struggle against
Fascism" after the Radicals had shown their complete inability to
struggle against Fascism. The parliamentary bloc with the Radicals, which was a crime from the point of view of the historical

LEON TROTSKY

The development which is taking place among the masses of the petty bourgeoisie has exceptional importance for an understanding of the political situation. The political crisis of the country is above all a collapse of the confidence of the petty bourgeois masses in their traditional parties and leaders. *The discontent, the nervousness, the instability, the fluidity of the petty bourgeoisie* are extremely important characteristics of a pre-revolutionary situation. As a sick man, burning with fever, tosses from right side to left, so the feverish petty bourgeoisie can turn to the Right or to the Left. In the coming period, the side towards which millions of French peasants, artisans, small merchants and minor officials turn will determine whether the present pre-revolutionary situation will develop into a revolutionary or a counter-revolutionary situation.

The alleviation of the economic crisis might—though not for long—retard, but not stop, the shifting of the petty bourgeoisie to the Right or the Left. On the other hand, if the crisis becomes intensified, the bankruptcy of Radical Socialism and of all the parliamentary groupings around it will proceed with redoubled speed.

It must not be thought that Fascism has to become a strong parliamentary party before it can take over power. This was the case in Germany, but not in Italy. In order that Fascism should succeed, it is not necessary that the petty bourgeoisie should break *beforehand* with the old "democratic" parties. It is enough if the petty bourgeoisie has lost its confidence in these parties, and looks uneasily about it for new roads.

In the next municipal elections the petty bourgeoisie may still give a large number of votes to the Radicals and similar groupings, in the absence of a new political party which could succeed in gaining the confidence of the peasants and

interests of the proletariat, had at least a certain practical value in the restricted domain of parliamentarianism. The extra-parliamentary alliance with the Radicals against Fascism is not merely a crime, but an idiocy.—L.T.

the urban middle classes. And, nevertheless, a Fascist military *coup*, with the aid of the big bourgeoisie, might take place a few months after the elections; and by its influence attract the sympathies of the most desperate layers of the petty bourgeoisie.

That is why it would be a serious illusion to take consolation in the thought that the Fascist banner has not yet become popular in the provinces and the villages. The anti-parliamentary tendencies of the petty bourgeoisie, after breaking away from the channel of the official parliamentary politics of the old parties, may directly and immediately support a military *coup d'état*, when that becomes necessary for the safety of finance capital. Such a method of action is most closely adapted to the traditions and temperament of France.*

The outcome of elections has, of course, a symptomatic importance. But to rely on this index *alone* would be to fall victim to parliamentary cretinism. We are dealing with much more profound processes which, one fine day, will catch our friends, the parliamentarians, off guard. Here, as in other matters, the question is settled not by arithmetic, but by the dynamics of the struggle. The big bourgeoisie does not register passively the evolution of the middle classes, but, rather, prepares tentacles of steel with which to seize these tortured and despairing masses at the opportune moment.

* * *

Marxist thought is *dialectical*; it considers all phenomena in their development, in their transition from one state to

---

* Marxism in no way ignores (let us remark in passing) such factors as tradition and national temperament. The fundamental direction of historical development is, of course, determined by the progress of the class struggle; but the *forms* of this development, its *rhythm*, etc., can vary a great deal under the influence of temperament and national tradition, which, themselves, have been formed in the past under the influence of the progress of the class struggle.—L.T.

another. The thought of the conservative petty bourgeois is *metaphysical*; its conceptions are fixed and immovable, and between phenomena it supposes that there are unbridgeable gaps. The absolute opposition of a revolutionary situation to a non-revolutionary situation is a classic example of metaphysical thought, according to the axiom: whatever is, is; whatever is not, is not; and anything else is the Devil's doing.

In the processes of history we find stable situations which are altogether non-revolutionary. We find likewise situations which are obviously revolutionary. And again, there are counter-revolutionary situations (we had better not forget them!). But the most striking features of our epoch of capitalism in decay are *intermediate* and *transitional*: situations between the non-revolutionary and the pre-revolutionary, between the pre-revolutionary and the revolutionary or . . . the counter-revolutionary. It is precisely these transitional stages which have a decisive importance from the point of view of political strategy.

What would we say about an artist who could distinguish only between the two opposite colors in the spectrum? That he had no sense of color or was half-blind, and that he ought to give up the easel. What will we say about a political strategist who can distinguish only between the two states: "revolutionary" and "non-revolutionary"? That he is not a Marxist, but a Stalinist, who might make a good functionary but never a proletarian leader.

A revolutionary situation develops out of the reciprocal action of objective and subjective factors. If the party of the proletariat is incapable of analyzing in time the tendencies of a pre-revolutionary situation we shall inevitably have a counter-revolutionary situation. *The French proletariat now faces this danger.* The shortsighted, passive, opportunist policies of the United Front—above all of the Stalinists, who have become its Right wing—are *the chief obstacle in the path of the proletarian revolution in France.*

ONCE AGAIN, WHITHER FRANCE?

2. IMMEDIATE DEMANDS AND THE STRUGGLE FOR POWER

The Central Committee of the Communist Party rejects the struggle for the nationalization of the means of production as a demand incompatible with the existence of the bourgeois state. But the Central Committee likewise rejects the struggle for power in order to create the workers' state. To these tasks it *opposes* a program of "immediate demands."

As a matter of fact the United Front now has no program at all. At the same time, the experiences of the Communist Party itself in the struggle for "immediate demands" has been of an extremely unfortunate character. All the speeches, articles and resolutions on the necessity of combating capitalism by strikes have up to now resulted in nothing, or almost nothing. In spite of the situation in the country, which is becoming more and more acute, the working class is in a state of *dangerous stagnation*.

The Central Committee of the Communist Party accuses everybody except itself of being guilty of this stagnation. We do not want to whitewash anybody. Our point of view is well known. But we believe that the *chief obstacle* on the path to the development of the revolutionary struggle right now is the one-sided, almost maniacal program of "immediate demands," which contradicts the whole situation. We wish now, at sufficient length, to throw some light on the considerations and the arguments of the Central Committee of the Communist Party. Not that these arguments are either serious or profound: on the contrary, they are miserable. But we are dealing with the question upon which the fate of the French proletariat depends.

The most authoritative document on the question of "immediate demands" is the programmatic resolution of the Central Committee of the Communist Party (see *l'Humanité*, Feb. 24, 1935). Let us examine this document.

The outline of the immediate demands is given in vague general terms: against wage cuts, for increased social insurance, for collective bargaining, "against inflation," etc. Nothing is said about the character that the struggle for these demands can and must have under the conditions of the present social crisis. However, every worker knows that with two millions of partially or wholly unemployed, the ordinary trade union struggle for collective bargaining is utopian. Under present conditions, in order to force the capitalists to make important concessions, we must *break their wills;* this can be done only by a revolutionary offensive. But a revolutionary offensive, which opposes one class to another, cannot be developed solely under slogans of partial economic demands. We have here a vicious circle. This is the principal reason for the stagnation of the United Front.

The general Marxist thesis, "Social reforms are only the by-products of the revolutionary struggle," has in the epoch of the decline of capitalism the most immediate and burning importance. The capitalists are able to cede *something* to the workers only if they are threatened with the danger of losing *everything.*

However, even the greatest "concessions" of which contemporary capitalism—itself in a blind alley—is capable are completely insignificant in comparison with the misery of the masses and the depth of the social crisis. This is why the most immediate of all demands must be for the *expropriation of the capitalists and the nationalization (socialization) of the means of production.* But is not this demand unrealizable under the rule of the bourgeoisie? Quite so! That is why we must seize power.

The resolution of the Central Committee recognizes in passing that "the party has not yet succeeded in organizing and extending the resistance to the offensive of capitalism," but the resolution does not stop at all to consider the question why, in spite of the efforts of the Communist Party

and the C.G.T.U.,* the successes in the defensive economic
struggles are completely insignificant. Millions of workers
and wage earners participated in the general strike of February 12, which did not make any "immediate demands."
However, up to the present, only a small fraction of this
number has participated in the defense against the offensive
of capitalism. Does not this astonishingly clear fact lead
the "leaders" of the Communist Party to draw any conclusion? Why is it that millions of workers risked participation in a general strike, in violent demonstrations in the
streets, in battles with the Fascist gangs, but refuse to participate in strikes of a purely economic character?

"We must understand," says the resolution, "the feelings
which agitate the workers, who want to proceed to action."
We must understand . . . but the misfortune is that the
authors of the resolution themselves understand nothing.
Whoever goes to workers' meetings knows as well as we that
general talk about immediate demands usually leaves the
audience in a state of complete indifference; on the other
hand, clear and precise revolutionary slogans get a sym-
pathetic response. This difference in the reaction of the
masses characterizes the political situation in the country
in the clearest possible manner.

"In the present period," the resolution unexpectedly
states, "the economic struggle requires *heavy sacrifices* on
the part of the workers." It ought to have added further:
and it is only in exceptional cases that the sacrifices promise
any positive results. However, the struggle for immediate
demands has for its task the *alleviation* of the condition of
the workers. By putting this economic struggle at the head
of the list and by renouncing revolutionary slogans for its
sake, the Stalinists no doubt believe that it is precisely the
partial economic struggle which can best arouse large
masses. The truth is just the opposite: the masses make

* Unified General Confederation of Labor, Stalinist dual union
organization which was merged with the much larger C.G.T. this
year.—TR.

hardly any response to appeals for strikes on a purely economic plane. In politics, how can anyone avoid facing the facts?

The masses understand or feel that, under the conditions of the crisis and of unemployment, partial economic conflicts require unheard of sacrifices which will never be justified in any case by the results obtained. The masses wait for and demand other and more efficacious methods. Messrs. strategists, learn from the masses: they are guided by a sure revolutionary instinct.

Basing themselves on badly assimilated citations from Lenin, the Stalinists repeat: "Strike struggles are possible even in times of crisis." They do not understand that there are crises and crises. In the epoch when capitalism was on the ascendant, both industrialists and workers, even during an acute crisis, looked forward toward the next boom period. *But the present crisis is the rule, not the exception.* On the purely *economic* level, the working class is thrown into a disorderly retreat by the terrific pressure of the economic catastrophe. On the other hand, the decline of capitalism, with all its weight, pushes the proletariat on the road toward the revolutionary mass struggle for *political* power. However, the leadership of the Communist Party tries with all its force to bar this road. Thus in the hands of the Stalinists the program of "immediate demands" becomes an instrument for the disorientation and disorganization of the proletariat. But *a political offensive* (a struggle for power) with an active defense army (militia) would at once alter the relationship of class forces and would at the same time, *even for the most backward layers of the working class,* open up the possibility for a victorious *economic struggle.*

Capitalism in its death-throes, as we know, also has its cycles, but these cycles are declining and diseased. Only the proletarian revolution can put an end to the crisis of the *capitalist system.* The *cyclical* crisis will inevitably give way to a new and brief upturn, if neither war nor revolution intervenes.

ONCE AGAIN, WHITHER FRANCE?

In case of an upturn in the business cycle, the strike struggles no doubt will have more extensive possibilities. This is why it is necessary to follow closely the movement of trade and industry, particularly the changes in employment, without capitulating to the meteorologists of the school of Jouhaux and all the while giving practical help to the workers in applying pressure to the capitalists at the necessary moment. But even in the case of extensive strike struggles it would be criminal to have them limited to partial economic demands. The upturn in the business cycle can be neither considerable nor of long duration, for we now are confronted with the cycle of a capitalism which is irremediably diseased. The new crisis, after a brief upturn, will be found to be more devastating than the present. All the fundamental problems will rise up anew with redoubled force and sharpness. If we lose time, the growth of Fascism will be found irresistible.

But today the economic upturn is no more than a hypothesis. The actuality is a deepening of the crisis, the two-year term of military service, the rearmament of Germany, the danger of war.

This actuality must be our point of departure.

* * *

The last idea in the programmatic resolution of the Central Committee worthily crowns the whole structure. Let us quote literally: "While fighting every day in order to relieve the toiling masses from the misery which the capitalist regime imposes upon them, the Communists *emphasize* that final emancipation can be gained only by the abolition of the capitalist regime and the setting up of the Dictatorship of the Proletariat." This formula did not sound so bad at the dawn of Social Democracy half a century or more ago. At that time, and not without success, the Social Democracy guided the struggle of the workers for immediate demands and isolated reforms, for what they called the "minimum program," all the time "emphasizing" that the *final* emancipation of the proletariat could be realized only by the revolution. The "final goal" of socialism was at that time seen across the cloudy distance of the years. It is this conception, which was completely outworn already at the beginning of the war, that the Central Committee of the Communist Party has unexpectedly transported into our epoch, repeating it word for word to the last comma. And these people invoke the names of Marx and Lenin!

When they "emphasize" that "the final emancipation" can be obtained only by the abolition of the capitalist regime, they manipulate this elementary truth in order to deceive the workers. For they give the workers the idea that a certain alleviation, even an important alleviation in their condition can be obtained within the framework of the present regime. They picture rotting and declining capitalism in the same way that their fathers and grandfathers pictured robust and ascending capitalism. The fact is indisputable: the Stalinists have taken over the refuse of reformism.

The Marxist political thesis must be the following: "While explaining constantly to the masses that rotting capitalism has no place either for the alleviation of their situation or even for the maintenance of their customary level of misery, while putting openly before the masses the tasks of the socialist revolution as the immediate task of our day, while mobilizing the workers for the conquest of power, while defending the workers' organizations with the help of the workers' militia,—the communists (or the socialists) will at the same time lose no opportunity to snatch this or that partial concession from the enemy, or at least to prevent the further lowering of the living standard of the workers."

Compare this thesis carefully with the lines cited above from the resolution of the Central Committee. The difference, we hope, is clear. In one instance, *Stalinism*; in the other, *Leninism*. Between them lies an abyss.

Higher wages, collective bargaining, against inflation. . . .

But what about unemployment? The resolution of the Central Committee will come to our help here also. Let us quote:

"They (the Communists) demand public works. To this end, they have elaborated specific proposals adapted to each local and regional situation, and have prescribed the means for financing them (a capital levy, government loans, etc. . . .)."

Isn't this astonishing? This charlatan's recipe is copied almost word for word from Jouhaux: the Stalinists reject the progressive demands of his "plan," and adopt the most fantastic and utopian parts.

The principal productive forces of society are paralyzed or half-paralyzed by the crisis. The workers are in a stupor before the machines which they have created. Our savior, the Central Committee, proposes: outside of the real capitalist economy, alongside it, we shall create another capitalist economy on the basis of "public works."

Don't let anyone tell us that we are dealing here with temporary undertakings: present unemployment does not have a temporary character; it is not merely cyclical unemployment, but structural unemployment, the most deadly expression of the decline of capitalism. To do away with it, the Central Committee proposes to create a system of public works adapted to each region of the country, with the help of a special system of financing, alongside of the disarranged finances of capitalism. In a word, the Central Committee of the Communist Party proposes quite simply that capitalism change its residence. And it is this "plan" that is counterposed to the struggle for power and a program of nationalization! *There are no worse opportunists than frightened adventurists.*

On the problem of how to get public works, a capital levy, government loans, etc., the resolution says not a word. No doubt, with the help of . . . petitions. This is the most opportune and the most efficacious method of action. Neither crises, nor Fascism, nor militarism, can put up a fight against petitions. Moreover, petitions will revive the paper industry, and thus relieve unemployment. Let us take note: the organization of petitions is a fundamental part of the system of public works, according to the plan of Thorez and company.

Whom are these people making fun of? Of themselves, or of the working class?

"It is astonishing that the proletariat endures passively such privations and such terror after a class struggle of more than a century." On every occasion we hear this lofty phrase from the mouth of a socialist or a communist in his study. Is there insufficient resistance? The blame is put on the backs of the working masses. As if the parties and the unions stood apart from the proletariat and were not its organs of struggle! It is precisely because the proletariat, as the result of its more than a century old struggles, has created its political and trade union organizations, that it is difficult and almost impossible for it to carry on the struggle against capitalism *without them* and *against them*. What was built as the main spring of action has become a dead weight, a brake.

The whole situation imbues the workers with the idea that revolutionary actions are necessary to change all the conditions of existence. But precisely because it is a question of a decisive struggle, which must include millions of men, the initiative naturally rests with the *directing organizations*, with the working class parties, with the United Front. From them must come a clear program, slogans, the mobilization for battle. In order to rouse the masses, the parties must themselves be aroused, and must launch a strenuous revolutionary campaign throughout the country. But the directing organizations, the Communist Party included, haven't the courage. The Communist Party tosses its tasks and its responsibilities on to the masses. It wants millions of men, left by it without revolutionary leadership, to engage in isolated struggles for partial demands and to show skeptical bureaucrats that they are ready to do battle.

ONCE AGAIN, WHITHER FRANCE?

Perhaps after that the big chiefs will consent to command an offensive. In place of *directing* the masses, the bureaucratic Central Committee *examines* the masses, flunks them, and thus justifies its own opportunism and cowardice.

During the time of relative economic and political stability in France (1929-1933), the Central Committee of the Communist Party proclaimed the "Third Period," and would not be satisfied with anything less than the conquest of the streets at the barricades. Now, at the time of the economic, social and political crisis, the same Central Committee is satisfied with a modest program of "immediate demands." This absurd contradiction is the complex product of many factors: fright at former errors, inability to understand the masses, the bureaucratic habit of laying down a blue print for the proletariat—and, finally, intellectual anarchy, the result of zigzags, falsifications, lies and repressions without number.

The first author of the new program is, no doubt, the present "leader" of the Comintern, Bela Kun, who goes day by day further on the road from adventurism to opportunism. After reading in Lenin that the Bolsheviks were for strikes *under certain conditions,* and the Mensheviks against them, in the wink of an eye Bela Kun founded his "realistic" policies on this discovery. But to his misfortune, Bela Kun had not opened Lenin . . . at the right page.

During certain periods, purely economic strike struggles did in fact play an enormous role in the revolutionary movement of the Russian proletariat. Now, Russian capitalism was not rotting at that time, but was growing and advancing rapidly. The Russian proletariat was a virgin class, and the strikes were for it the first form of awakening and activity. Finally, the extensive spread of the strikes coincided each time with a rise in the business cycle.

None of these conditions exists in France. The proletariat has behind it a mighty schooling of revolution, of trade union and parliamentary struggle, with the whole positive and negative heritage of this rich past. From this, one would hardly expect a spontaneous strike wave in France, even in a period of a rise in the business cycle, and still more so while the cyclical crisis deepens the misery of declining capitalism.

The other side of the question is not less important. At the time of the first impetuous strike wave in Russia, there was only a single fraction of the Russian Social-Democracy which tried to restrict it to partial economic demands: this was the group called the "Economists." In their opinion, it was necessary to reject the slogan, "Down with Autocracy!" until the appearance of a "revolutionary situation." Lenin thought that the "Economists" were miserable opportunists. He showed that *a revolutionary situation must be actively prepared*, even during a strike movement.

In general, it is absurd to try to carry over mechanically into France the various stages and episodes of the Russian revolutionary movement. But it is even more absurd to do it after the manner of Bela Kun, who understands neither Russia, nor France, nor Marxism. In the school of Lenin, we must learn *the method of action*, and not try to change Leninism into citations and recipes, good for every occasion in life.

* * *

Thus, the situation in France, in the opinion of the Stalinists, is not revolutionary; revolutionary slogans, on this analysis, are out of place; we must concentrate all attention on economic strikes and on partial demands. This is the program. It is an opportunist and a lifeless program, but still, it's a program.

Alongside it there is, however, another. *L'Humanité* repeats every day the triple slogan: "Peace, Bread, Freedom." It was under this slogan, *l'Humanité* explains, that the Bolsheviks conquered in 1917. Following the example of the Stalinists, Just repeats the same idea. Very good. But in 1917, in Russia, there was a situation notoriously revolutionary. How then can this slogan, which assured the success of the proletarian revolution, be any good along

with "immediate demands" in a non-revolutionary situation?
Let the seers of *l'Humanité* explain this mystery to us
simple mortals.

On our part, we recall that "immediate demands" rein-
forced the triple slogan of the Bolsheviks.

"For Peace." That meant in 1917, under the war conditions, struggle against all the patriotic parties from the
monarchists to the Mensheviks, the demand for the publica-
tion of the secret treaties, the revolutionary mobilization of
the soldiers against the General Staff, and fraternization at
the front. "For Peace!" That meant defiance of the militarism of Austria and Germany on one side, and of the Allies
on the other. The slogan of the Bolsheviks thus meant the
most daring and revolutionary policy ever known in the
history of mankind.

To "struggle" for peace in 1935, in alliance with Herriot
and the bourgeois "pacifists" (that is to say, the hypocrit-
ical imperialists), means simply to uphold the *status quo*,
which is satisfactory at the present moment to the French
bourgeoisie. It means to put the workers to sleep and to
demoralize them with illusions about "disarmament" and
"non-aggression pacts," with the lie of the League of Nations, while preparing a new capitulation of the working
class parties at the moment when the French bourgeoisie or
its rivals choose to upset the *status quo*.

"For Bread!" That meant for the Bolsheviks in 1917
the *expropriation of the land and of the grain reserves belonging to the landlords and speculators, and the monopoly
of the grain trade in the hands of the workers' and peasants'
government.* What does "For Bread!" mean to the Stalinists in 1935? A mere verbal formula!

"For Freedom!" The Bolsheviks showed the masses that
freedom was an illusion while schools, press and meeting
halls remained in the hands of the bourgeoisie. "For Freedom!" meant: the seizure of power by the Soviets, the expropriation of the landlords, workers' control of production.

"For Freedom!" in alliance with Herriot and the old

ladies of both sexes in the League for the Rights of Man
means to uphold the semi-Bonapartist, semi-parliamentarian
government, and that is all it can mean. The bourgeoisie
needs right now not only the gangs of la Rocque, but likewise the "Left" reputation of Herriot. Finance-capital is
busy arming the Fascists. The Stalinists are restoring the
Left reputation of Herriot with the help of the masquerading
"People's Front." This is what the slogans of the October
Revolution are used for in 1935!

As the single example of the new style "realistic" policies,
the resolution of the Central Committee tells how the unemployed of Villejuif are eating the Croix de Feu's soup, and
yelling: "To the stake with la Rocque!" How many are
eating soup and how many yelling, they don't tell us: the
Stalinists are never able to endure figures. But that is not
the question. . . . To what point has a "revolutionary" party
fallen when, in a programmatic resolution, it can find no
other example of proletarian policies than the impotent yells
of harrassed and starving workers, forced to nourish themselves on the crumbs of Fascist philanthropy? And these
leaders feel neither humiliated nor ashamed!

Once, while talking about certain of his disciples, Marx
quoted the words of Heine: "I have sown dragons, and I
have harvested fleas." We are very much afraid that the
founders of the Third International will have to repeat
these same words. . . . However, our epoch needs not fleas,
but dragons.

3. The Struggle Against Fascism and the
General Strike

The program of the Communist International, written in
1928, during the period of the theoretical decline of the
C. I., states, "The epoch of imperialism is the epoch of
capitalism in its death throes." By itself, this statement,
which was formulated by Lenin a long time ago, is absolutely incontestable, and is of decisive importance for the

policies of the proletariat in our epoch. But the authors of the program of the Communist International failed utterly to understand the thesis on capitalism in its *death throes* or *in decay,* which they had mechanically adopted. This lack of comprehension stands revealed with especial clarity in respect to what is to us the most burning question, namely, Fascism.

The program of the Communist International has the following to say on this subject: *"Side by side* with the Social Democracy which assists the bourgeoisie to stifle the proletariat and to lull its vigilance, Fascism appears." The Communist International failed to understand that it is not the mission of Fascism to function *side by side* with the Social Democracy, but to destroy all the existing workers' organizations, including the reformist. The task of Fascism, in the words of the program, is to "annihilate the *communist* strata of the proletariat, and their leading cadres." Fascism, then, does not at all threaten the Social Democracy and the reformist trade-unions; on the contrary, the Social Democracy itself plays a "Fascist" role to an ever increasing degree. Fascism achieves nothing more than the consummation of the labors of reformism, by functioning *"side by side* with the Social Democracy."

We are quoting not from an article by some Thorez or Duclos who contradicts himself at every step, but from the basic document of the Communist International, its program. (See Chapter II, paragraph 3: "The Crisis of Capitalism and Fascism.") We have here before us all the basic elements of the theory of *social Fascism.* The leaders of the Communist International failed to understand that capitalism in decay is no longer able to come to terms with the most moderate and most servile Social Democracy, either as a party in power, or as a party in opposition. It is the mission of Fascism to take its place not "side by side with the Social Democracy," but on its bones. Precisely from this there flows the possibility, the need and the urgency for the united front. But the miserable leadership of the Communist International made no attempt to apply the policy of the united front except during the period when it could not be forced upon the Social Democracy. As soon as the position of reformism was shaken, and when the Social Democracy began to fall under blows, the Communist International rejected the united front. These people have the grievous habit of wearing their overcoats in the summer and of venturing out in the winter without so much as a fig-leaf!

Despite the instructive experience of Italy, the Communist International inscribed on its banner the genial aphorism of Stalin, "Social Democracy and Fascism are not opposites, they are twins." Herein lies the main cause for the defeat of the German proletariat. True, the C. I. has made a sharp turn on the question of the united front: facts proved themselves more potent than the program. But the program of the Communist International has been neither suppressed, nor modified. Its fundamental mistakes have not been explained to the workers. The leaders of the Communist International, who have lost confidence in themselves, are preserving *against possible eventualities* an avenue of retreat towards the position of "social Fascism." This has invested the policy of the united front with its unprincipled, diplomatic and unstable character.

The inability to understand the meaning of Lenin's thesis on "capitalism in its death throes" has invested the present policies of the French Communist Party with its character of noisy impotence, supplemented by reformist illusions. Although Fascism represents the organic product of capitalist decay, the Stalinists have suddenly become convinced of the possibility of putting an end to Fascism without touching the foundations of bourgeois society.

On March 6, Thorez wrote for the one hundredth time in *l'Humanité*:

"In order to assure the *decisive* defeat of Fascism, we again propose to the Socialist Party joint action in defense of immediate demands. . . ."

ONCE AGAIN, WHITHER FRANCE?

Every class conscious worker must ponder well this "programmatic" phrase. Fascism, as we know, is born out of the union between the despair of the middle classes and the terrorist policy of big capital. The "immediate demands" are those demands which do not transcend the framework of capitalism. How, then, by remaining upon the arena of capitalism in decay, is it possible to "assure the decisive (!) defeat" of Fascism?

When Jouhaux says that by putting an end to the crisis (easier said than done!) we shall by this very thing vanquish Fascism, Jouhaux, at least, remains faithful to himself: he is again as always the watchdog of the hopes in the regeneration and rejuvenation of capitalism. But the Stalinists recognize, verbally, the inevitability of the progressive degeneration of capitalism. How, then, can they promise to render the political superstructure healthy, by assuring the decisive defeat of Fascism, and at the same time leave intact the decaying economic base of society?

Do they suppose that big capital is capable of turning the wheels of history back at its whim, and once again resuming the road of concessions and "reforms"? Do they think that the petty bourgeoisie can be saved by means of "immediate demands" from growing ruin, from being declassed and from despair? And how then to reconcile these trade union and reformist illusions with the thesis on capitalism in its death throes?

Taken on the theoretical plane, the position of the Communist Party sums up, as we have seen, to a most complete absurdity. Let us see how this position appears in the light of the actual struggle.

* * *

On February 28, Thorez expressed in the following words this very same central and radically false idea of the present policies of the Communist Party:

"To beat down Fascism decisively, it is necessary to put a halt, in no uncertain terms, to the economic offensive of capitalism against the living standards of the toiling masses."

Why then the workers' militia? What need of a direct struggle against Fascism? We must strive to raise the living standards of the masses, and Fascism will disappear, as if by magic.

Alas, along these lines, the entire perspective of the struggle immediately ahead is completely distorted, and the actual relationships are turned topsy-turvy. The capitalists arrive at Fascism not at their own whim, but through necessity: they cannot any longer preserve the private ownership of the means of production save by directing an offensive against the workers, save by strengthening the oppression, by sowing misery and despair around them. At the same time, fearing the inevitable resistance on the part of the workers, the capitalists, through the medium of their agents, arouse the petty bourgeoisie against the proletariat and, while accusing the latter of prolonging and aggravating the crisis, they finance Fascist gangs to annihilate the workers. Should the resistance of the workers to the offensive of capital increase on the morrow, should the strikes become more frequent and important, Fascism, despite what Thorez says, will not evaporate but instead grow with redoubled force. The growth of the strike movement will impel the mobilization of strike-breakers. All the "patriotic" thugs will participate in the movement. Daily attacks against the workers will be put on the order of the day. To close our eyes to this is to walk toward certain defeat.

Do you mean to say, Thorez and his colleagues will demand, that there must be no resistance? (And they will append the customary insults addressed to us, which we pass by as we would a cesspool.) No. It is necessary to resist.

We are no adherents of that school which thinks that the best means of safety lies in silence, retreat and capitulation. "Don't provoke the enemy!" "Do not defend yourselves!" "Don't arm yourselves!" "Roll over on your backs and play dead!" Theoreticians from among this school of strategy should be sought not among ourselves but among the editors of *l'Humanité!* It is necessary for the workers to resist, if they do not wish to be annihilated. But in that case no reformist and pacifist illusion is permissible. The struggle will be ferocious. It is necessary to foresee beforehand the inevitable consequences of resistance and to prepare for them.

By its present offensive the bourgeoisie invests with a *new* and incommensurably more acute character the relation between the economic conditions and the social situation of capitalism in decay. Just so, the workers must invest *their defense with a new character which corresponds to* the methods of the class enemy. In defending ourselves against the economic blows of capital, we must know how to defend at the same time our organizations against the mercenary gangs of capital. It is impossible to do this save by means of the *workers' militia.* No verbal assertions, no shrieks, no insult on the part of *l'Humanité* can invalidate this conclusion.

In particular we must say to the trade unions: comrades, your locals and your publications will be pillaged, your organizations reduced to dust, if you do not immediately proceed to the formation of *trade union defense squads* ("trade union militia"), if you do not demonstrate by actions that you will not surrender a single inch to Fascism without a struggle.

* * *

In the same article (Feb. 28), Thorez laments:

"The Socialist Party has not accepted our proposals for wide scale action, including the *strike,* against the decree-laws which are being ever more enforced."

Including the strike? What strike? Since the abolition of the decree-laws is involved here, what Thorez apparently has in view are not partial economic strikes but a general strike, that is to say, a political strike. He does not utter the words "general strike" in order not to make it obvious that he is repeating our long-standing proposal. To what humiliating subterfuges must these poor people resort in order to mask their vacillations and contradictions!

This procedure has become, it seems, a method. In the open letter of March 12, the Central Committee of the Communist Party proposed to the Socialist Party to inaugurate a decisive campaign against the two-year term of military service, "through all methods available, including the *strike.*" Once again the same mystic formula! The Central Committee has in mind evidently the strike as an instrument of political struggle, that is to say, as a revolutionary weapon. But why then does it fear to utter aloud the word general strike and simply speak of "a strike"? With whom is the Central Committee playing hide and seek? Is it with the proletariat, or no?

But putting aside these unbecoming maneuvers to maintain "prestige," there remains the fact that the Central Committee of the Communist Party proposes the general strike for the struggle against the Bonapartist legislation of Doumergue-Flandin. With this we are in full accord. But we demand that the leaders of working class organizations themselves understand and explain to the masses the meaning of the general strike under the present conditions as well as how it must be prepared.

Even an ordinary economic strike requires as a rule a militant organization, specifically, *pickets.* Under the present aggravated conditions of the class struggle, faced with the Fascist provocation and terror, a real organization of pickets is the essential prerequisite for all important economic struggles. Let us imagine, however, that some trade union leader would assert, "*Pickets* are not necessary, that would be a provocation—*self-defense* will suffice the strikers!" Isn't it obvious that the workers would amiably advise such a "leader" to go to a hospital; if not directly to an insane asylum? The fact is that pickets are precisely the most important organ of self-defense of the strikers!

Let us view more closely the line of reasoning relating to the general strike. We have in mind not an ordinary demonstration, nor a symbolic strike of an hour's or even 24 hours' duration, but a war maneuver, with the aim of forcing the enemy to submit. It is not difficult to understand what a terrific aggravation of the class struggle the general strike would imply under the present conditions! The Fascist gangs would sprout on all sides like mushrooms after a rain and they would attempt with all their might to bring confusion, provocation and demoralization among the ranks of the strikers. How else can we guard the general strike against needless sacrifices and even against complete annihilation if not by means of military and strictly disciplined workers' detachments? *The general strike is the generalization of the partial strike. The workers' militia is the generalization of the picket squads.* Only windbags and pathetic braggards can play with the idea of the general strike under the present conditions, and refuse at the same time to carry on the stubborn work for the creation of the workers' militia!

But the wretched members of the Central Committee of the Communist Party do not stop with this.

The general strike, as every Marxist knows, is one of the most revolutionary methods of struggle. The general strike is not possible except at a time when the class struggle rises above particular and craft demands, and extends over all occupational and district divisions, and wipes away the lines and the parties, between legality and illegality, and mobilizes the majority of the proletariat in an active opposition to the bourgeoisie and the state. Nothing can be on a higher plane than the general strike, except the armed insurrection. The entire history of the working class movement proves that every general strike, whatever may be the slogans under which it occurs, has an internal tendency to transform itself into an open revolutionary clash, into a direct struggle for power. In other words: the general strike is not possible except under the conditions of extreme political tension, and that is why it is always the incontestable expression of the revolutionary character of the situation. How then can the Central Committee propose a general strike in this case? "The situation is not a revolutionary one!"

Might not Thorez perhaps retort that he had in mind not a real general strike, but a little strike, quite peaceful, just exactly suited to the personal requirements of the editors of *l'Humanité*? Or perhaps may he not add discreetly that, foreseeing the refusal of the leaders of the S.F.I.O., he risks nothing by proposing a general strike to them? But most probably Thorez, in refutation, will merely accuse us of entering into a conspiracy with Chiappe, ex-Alphonso XIII and the Pope: this is the sort of rejoinder that suits Thorez best!

But every communist worker, who has a head on his shoulders, must ponder over the crying contradictions of his hapless leaders: it is impossible, you see, to build workers' militias because the situation is not revolutionary, it is impossible even to carry on propaganda in favor of the arming of the proletariat, that is to say, of preparing the workers for a revolutionary situation in the future; but it is possible, it appears, even today to call the workers to a general strike despite the absence of a revolutionary situation. In truth, we find transcended here all the boundaries of giddiness and absurdity!

At all meetings we hear the Communists repeating the slogan which they have inherited from the "Third Period" —"Soviets Everywhere!" It is absolutely clear that this slogan, if one takes it seriously, bears a profoundly revolutionary character: it is impossible to establish the Soviet regime otherwise than by means of an armed insurrection against the bourgeoisie. But an *armed* insurrection presupposes *arms* in the hands of the proletariat. Thus the slogan of "Soviets everywhere" and the slogan of "arming the workers" are intimately and indissolubly bound with one another. Why then is the former slogan being incessantly reiterated by the Stalinists while the latter is proclaimed a "Trotskyist provocation"?

ONCE AGAIN, WHITHER FRANCE?

Our bewilderment is all the more legitimate since the slogan of arming the workers most closely corresponds to the present political situation and the state of mind of the proletariat. The slogan of "Soviets" is, by its very essence, offensive in character and presupposes a victorious revolution. The proletariat, however, finds itself today in a defensive situation. Fascism threatens it directly with physical annihilation. The necessity for defense, even with arms in hand, is actually more comprehensive and more within the grasp of the widest strata of the masses than the idea of a revolutionary offensive. Thus the slogan of arming could at the present stage count upon a response much greater and much more active than the slogan of Soviets. How then could a working class party, unless it has really betrayed the interests of the revolution, let slip so exceptional an opportunity and so dishonestly compromise the idea of arming instead of ardently popularizing it?

We are ready to allow that our question is prompted by our "counter-revolutionary" nature, in particular, by our hopes of provoking military intervention; everyone knows that as soon as the Mikado and Hitler become convinced by our question that air currents are whistling through the heads of Bela Kun and Thorez, they will declare war against the U.S.S.R.

All this has been irrefutably established by Duclos and needs no proof. But all the same, deign to reply: how can one come to Soviet power without an armed insurrection? How can one come to an insurrection without arming the workers? How can one defend himself against Fasicsm without arms? How can we achieve armament, even partial, without propaganda for this slogan?

* * *

But is the general strike possible in the immediate future? To a question of this sort there is no *a priori* answer possible, that is to say, none ready made. To obtain an answer it is necessary to know how to question. Whom? The masses. How question them? By means of agitation.

Agitation is not only the means of communicating to the masses this or that slogan, calling the masses to action, etc. For a party, agitation is also a means of lending an ear to the masses, of sounding out its moods and thoughts, and reaching this or another decision in accordance with the results. Only the Stalinists have transformed agitation into a noisy monologue. For the Marxists, the Leninists, *agitation is always a dialogue with the masses*.

But in order that this dialogue give the necessary results, the party must estimate correctly the general situation within the country and outline the general course of the immediate struggle. By means of agitation and probing of the masses, the party must bring into its concepts the necessary corrections and exactitude, particularly in everything relating to the *rhythm of the movement and the dates for major actions*.

The situation in the country has been described above; it bears a pre-revolutionary character along with the non-revolutionary character of the leadership of the proletariat. And since the policy of the proletariat is the principal factor in the development of a revolutionary situation, the non-revolutionary character of the proletarian leadership checks the transformation of the pre-revolutionary situation into an open revolutionary situation and by this very thing contributes toward transforming it into a counter-revolutionary situation.

In objective reality there are, of course, no sharp boundaries between the different stages of the political process. One stage interpenetrates with another, and as a result of this the situation reveals various contradictions. These contradictions certainly make diagnosis and prognosis more difficult but they do not at all make it impossible.

The forces of the French proletariat remain not only unexhausted, but are indeed still intact. Fascism as a political factor among the petty bourgeois masses is relatively feeble as yet (much more powerful, nevertheless, than it seems to the parliamentarians). These two very important political facts allow us to say with firm conviction: nothing has been lost as yet, the possibility for transforming the pre-revolutionary situation into a revolutionary situation is still entirely open.

But in a capitalist country such as this there can be no revolutionary struggles without the general strike: if working men and women remain in the factories during the decisive days, who then will do the fighting? Thus, the general strike is on the order of the day.

But the question of the *moment* for the general strike is the question of knowing whether the masses are prepared to struggle and whether the workers' organizations are ready to lead them to battle.

Is it true, however, that the only thing lacking is the revolutionary leadership? Does not there exist a great force for conservatism within the masses themselves, within the proletariat? Such voices are raised from different sides. And there is nothing astonishing about it! When a revolutionary crisis approaches, many leaders, fearful of the responsibilities, hide themselves behind the pseudo-conservatism of the masses. History has taught us how a few weeks, even a few days prior to the October insurrection, such distinguished Bolsheviks as Zinoviev, Kamenev and Rykov (it is needless to mention such people as Losovsky, Manuilsky, etc.) asserted that the masses were worn out, and did not want to fight. And yet as revolutionists, Zinoviev, Kamenev and Rykov tower in stature far above the Cachins, Thorezes and Monmousseaus.

Whoever declares that the proletariat does not want to wage or is incapable of waging a revolutionary struggle, himself spreads calumny by ascribing his own feebleness and his own cowardice to the toiling masses. *Up to the present moment there has been not a single case either in Paris or the provinces where the masses remained deaf to a call from above.*

The greatest example in point is the general strike of February 12, 1934. Despite the complete division of the leadership, the lack of any serious preparation, the tenacious efforts of the leaders of the C.G.T. to reduce the movement to a minimum, since they could not evade it altogether, the general strike achieved the greatest success possible under the given conditions. It is clear that the masses want to struggle. Every class conscious worker must say to himself that the pressure from below must have been extremely powerful if Jouhaux himself had to bestir for a moment out of his immobility. True, involved here was not a general strike in the proper meaning of the term, but only a 24-hour demonstration. But this restriction was *not* put by the *masses*; it was dictated from *above*.

The demonstration of February 10 of this year in the Place de la République confirms the very same conclusion. The only weapon which the leading centers utilized to prepare for it was the cold water bucket. The only slogan which the masses heard was, "Hush! Hush!" And nevertheless the number of demonstrators surpassed all expectations. In the provinces things have been and remain during the past year in exactly the same state. It is impossible to adduce a single serious fact that would prove that the leaders wanted to struggle and the masses refused to follow them. Always and everywhere just the reverse relationship is to be observed. It preserves its full force even today. The rank and file want to fight, the tops apply the brake. It is here that the chief danger lies and it *may* end in a real catastrophe.

The same relationship is to be found not only between the parties (or the trade unions) and the proletariat but also within each of the parties. Thus Frossard has not the least support among the rank and file in the S.F.I.O.; the only ones who support him are the deputies and the mayors who want everything to remain as in the past. On the other hand, Marceau Pivert, thanks to his stand which is becoming more and more clear and resolute, has become one of the most popular figures with the rank and file. We recognize this all the more readily since we have never renounced in the past, as we shall not refrain in the future, from speaking out openly when we are not in agreement with Pivert.*

Taken as a political symptom this fact by its importance far transcends the question of personalities of Frossard and Pivert: it indicates the general tendency of development. *The rank and file of the Socialist Party, as of the Communist Party, is more to the Left, more revolutionary, more audacious than the upper crust*: this is precisely why it is ready to place confidence only in the Left wing leaders. Still more: it is pushing the sincere Socialist always further to the Left. Why does the rank and file itself become radicalized? Because it finds itself in direct contact with the masses of the population, with their misery, their revolt and their hatred. This is an infallible symptom. We can rely on it.

The leaders of the Communist Party can, indeed, cite the fact that the masses failed to respond to their appeals. But this fact does not invalidate, instead it confirms our analysis. The working masses understand what the "leaders" do not understand, that is to say, that under the conditions of a very great social crisis, a partial economic struggle alone, which requires enormous efforts and enormous sacrifices, can not achieve any serious results. Worse yet, it can weaken and exhaust the proletariat. The workers are ready to participate in fighting demonstrations and even in a general strike but not in petty, exhausting strikes, without any perspective. Despite the appeals, manifestoes and articles in *l'Humanité*, the communist agitators hardly appear at all before the masses to preach strikes in the

---

* After moving Leftward for a time under the influence of the Trotskyists in the Left wing of the S.F.I.O. (French Socialist Party), Marceau Pivert stopped midway, failing to put up any struggle against the expulsion of the Trotskyists for advocating revolutionary defeatism and the slogan of the workers' militia. Pivert made his peace with the party bureaucracy and remained inside the party as a "Left" cover for the People's Front betrayal. When Blum assumed power as premier in a coalition government, Pivert gave him full support, stating that all that was left now to achieve was organic unity with the Stalinists!—Tr.

name of "partial immediate demands." They sense that the bureaucratic plans of their leaders do not correspond at all either to the objective situation or the mood of the masses. Without great perspectives, the masses cannot and will not begin to struggle. The policy of *l'Humanité* is the policy of an artificial and false pseudo-"realism." The failure of the C.G.T.U. in calling partial strikes is the indirect but very actual confirmation of the profundity of the crisis and of the moral tension in the workers' districts.

One should not think, however, that the radicalization of the masses will proceed by itself, automatically. The working class waits for initiative on the part of its organizations. When it arrives at the conclusion that its expectations have been false—and this moment is, perhaps, not so very distant—the process of radicalization will break off and be transformed into manifestations of discouragement, apathy and isolated explosions of despair. At the periphery of the proletariat, anarchist tendencies impinge upon Fascist tendencies. The wine will turn to vinegar.

The shifts in the political mood of the masses demand the greatest attention possible. To probe this living dialectic at every stage—that is the task of agitation. So far, the United Front criminally continues to lag behind the development of the social crisis and the mood of the masses. It is still possible to make up for lost time. But we must not lose any more time. Today history is to be reckoned not in terms of years, but in months and weeks.

* * *

To determine to what degree the masses are ripe for the general strike and at the same time to strengthen the militant mood of the masses, it is necessary to place before them a program of revolutionary action. Partial slogans such as the abolition of the Bonapartist decree-laws and of the two-year term of military service will find, of course, an important place in such a program. But these two episodic slogans are entirely inadequate.

Above all the tasks and partial demands of our epoch

there stands the *QUESTION OF POWER.* Since February
6, 1934, the question of power has been openly posed as a
question of armed force. The municipal and parliamentary
elections can be of importance insofar as the evaluation of
forces is concerned—but nothing more. The question will
be settled by the open conflict between the two camps. Governments of the type of Doumergue-Flandin, etc., occupy the
forefront only up to the day of the decisive climax. On the
morrow, either Fascism or the proletariat will govern
France.

It is precisely because the present intermediate state regime is extremely unstable, that the general strike *can*
achieve very great partial successes by forcing the government to take to the road of concessions on the question of
the Bonapartist decree-laws, the two-year term of military
service, etc. But such a success, extremely valuable and
important in itself, will not re-establish the equilibrium of
"democracy": finance capital will redouble its subsidies
to Fascism, and the question of power, perhaps after a brief
interlude, will be posed with redoubled force.

The fundamental importance of the general strike, independent of the partial successes which it may and then
again may not provide, lies in the fact that it poses the
question of power in a revolutionary manner. By shutting
down the factories, transport, generally all the means of
communication, power stations, etc., the proletariat by this
very act paralyzes not only production but also the government. The state power remains suspended in mid-air. It
must either subjugate the proletariat by famine and force
and constrain it to set the apparatus of the bourgeois state
once again in motion, or retreat before the proletariat.

Whatever may be the slogans and the motive for which
the general strike is initiated, if it includes the genuine
masses, and if these masses are quite resolved to struggle,
the general strike inevitably poses before all the classes in the
nation the question: *Who will be the master of the house?*
The leaders of the proletariat must understand this in-

ternal logic of the general strike, unless they are not leaders but dilettantes and adventurers. Politically this implies that from now on the leaders will continue to pose before the proletariat the task of the revolutionary conquest of power. If not, they must not venture to speak of the general strike. But by renouncing the general strike, they renounce thereby all revolutionary struggle, that is to say, they betray the proletariat to Fascism.

Either complete capitulation or revolutionary struggle for power—such is the alternative which flows from all the conditions of the present crisis. Whoever has not understood this alternative, has no business in the camp of the proletariat.

*　　*　　*

The question of the general strike is complicated by the fact that the C.G.T. proclaims that it has a monopoly on declaring and conducting the general strike. From this it follows that this question does not at all concern the working class parties. And at first sight, what is most astonishing is that there are to be found socialist parliamentarians who consider this claim to be quite in order: in reality, they merely wish to rid themselves of the responsibility.

The general strike, as the name itself already indicates, has for its goal the inclusion, in so far as it is possible, of the entire proletariat. The C.G.T. includes in its ranks probably not more than 5 to 8% of the proletariat. The influence of the C.G.T. itself outside the confines of the trade unions is absolutely insignificant to the extent that on general questions it does not equal the influence of the working class parties. Is it possible, for example, to compare the influence of *Le Peuple* to the influence of *Le Populaire* or *l'Humanité?*

The leadership of the C.G.T., in its conceptions and methods, is incomparably still further away from the tasks of the present epoch than the leadership of the working class parties. The lower one passes from the upper crust of the apparatus to the rank and file of the trade unions, the less confidence one finds in Jouhaux and his group. The lack of confidence changes more and more into open distrust. The present conservative apparatus of the C.G.T. will be inevitably swept away by the subsequent development of the revolutionary crisis.

The general strike is, by its very essence, a political act. It opposes the working class, as a whole, to the bourgeois state. It assembles together union and non-union workers, socialists, communists and non-party men. It requires an apparatus with a press and agitators such as the C.G.T. alone does not have at its disposal.

The general strike poses directly the question of the conquest of power by the proletariat. The C.G.T. has turned and is turning its back on this task (the leaders of the C.G.T. turn their faces towards the bourgeois power). The leaders of the C.G.T. themselves know that the leadership of the general strike is beyond their forces. If they, nevertheless, proclaim their monopoly to direct it, it is solely because they hope in this way to stifle the general strike even before its birth.

And what about the general strike of February 12, 1934? It was only a brief and peaceful demonstration imposed upon the C.G.T. by the socialist and communist workers. Jouhaux and his colleagues themselves took over the nominal leadership of the resistance precisely in order to prevent it from transforming itself into a revolutionary general strike.

In its instructions to its propagandists, the C.G.T. said, "On the morrow after February 6th, the laboring population and *all the democratic elements*, at the appeal of the C.G.T., demonstrated their firm will to bar the road to the *factionalists*. On its own part, the C.G.T. took note neither of the socialists nor of the communists—only of the "democrats." In this single phrase, Jouhaux is summed up. That is precisely why it would be criminal to place confidence in Jouhaux to decide the question of knowing whether it should or should not be a revolutionary struggle.

Of course in the preparation and conduct of the general strike, the trade unions will play a very influential role; yet not by virtue of a monopoly, but side by side with the working class parties. From the revolutionary standpoint it is particularly important to collaborate intimately with *local* trade union organizations without the slightest injury, of course, to their autonomy. As regards the C.G.T., it will either take its place in the common proletarian front by cutting away from the "democrats," or remain on the sidelines. Shall we co-operate loyally with equal rights? Yes! Shall we decide jointly the time and the methods of conducting the general strike? Yes! Shall we recognize Jouhaux's monopoly to stifle the revolutionary movement? Never!

4. SOCIALISM AND ARMED STRUGGLE

On February 6, 1935, the Fascist Leagues prepared to demonstrate on the Place de la Concorde. And what did the United Front and, in particular, the Central Committee of the Communist Party do? It called the workers of Paris to demonstrate at the Place de la Concorde at the same time as the Fascists. Were the Fascists perhaps to be without arms? No. After a year's time they were armed twofold. Did the Central Committee of the Communist Party propose adequately to arm the defense squads? Oh, no. The Central Committee is against "putchism" and "physical struggle." How, then, is it possible to throw tens of thousands of workers without arms, without preparation, without defense, against Fascist gangs excellently drilled and armed who bear a bloody hatred towards the revolutionary proletariat?

Let no malicious people tell us that the Central Committee of the Communist Party did not want to place the workers under the guns of the Fascists; that its sole desire was to give Flandin a convenient pretext to prohibit the Fascist demonstration. For that is worse yet. The Central Committee of the Communist Party, it then appears, gambled with the heads of the workers, and the outcome of this gamble depended entirely upon Flandin, more exactly upon the chiefs of police from the school of Chiappe. And what would have been the outcome had the police prefecture decided to profit by the excellent occasion and teach the revolutionary workers a lesson through the medium of the Fascists, moreover making responsibility for the butchery fall upon the leaders of the United Front? It is not difficult to imagine the consequences! While no bloody massacre resulted this particular time, in the event of the continuation of the same policy, it will result inevitably and infallibly, upon the next similar occasion.

The conduct of the Central Committee was the purest form of bureaucratic adventurism. Marxists have always taught that *opportunism and adventurism are two sides of one and the same coin.* February 6, 1935 has shown us with remarkable clarity how easily the coin may be reversed.

"We are against putchism, against insurrectionism!" Otto Bauer used to repeat year after year and spared no effort to rid himself of the Schutzbund (Workers' Militia) which was left as a heritage by the 1918 revolution. The powerful Austrian Social Democracy retreated in a cowardly manner, it adapted itself to the bourgeoisie, it retreated again, issued foolish "petitions," created a false appearance of struggle, placed its hopes upon its own Flandin (his name was Dollfuss), surrendered position after position and when it saw itself at the bottom of abyss it began to shriek hysterically, "Workers, to the rescue!" The best militants, without any contact with the masses who were disoriented, overwhelmed and duped, threw themselves into the struggle and suffered an inevitable defeat. After which, Otto Bauer and Julius Deutsch declared, "*We* behaved like revolutionaries but the *proletariat* did not support us!"

The events in Spain unfolded after a similar pattern. The Social Democratic leaders called the workers to an insurrection after they had surrendered to the bourgeoisie all the conquered revolutionary positions, and after they had exhausted the popular masses by their policy of retreat. The professional "anti-putchists" found themselves compelled to call for armed defense under such conditions as invested it to a large degree with the character of a "putsch."

February 6, 1935 was a minor repetition in France of the events in Austria and Spain. During the course of several months the Stalinists lulled and demoralized the workers, they ridiculed the slogan for the militia and "rejected" the physical struggle. Then all of a sudden, without the slightest preparation they commanded the proletariat, "To the Place de la Concorde. Forward, march!" This time, the good Langeron saved them. But if on the morrow, when the atmosphere will become hotter still, the Fascist thugs should assassinate scores of workers' leaders or set fire to *l'Humanité*—who will declare that this is improbable?— the wise Central Committee will infallibly shriek out, "Workers, to arms!" And then, either when committed to a concentration camp, or while promenading along the streets of London, if they get that far, the same leaders will haughtily declare, "We called for the insurrection, but the workers did not support us!"

The secret of success, obviously, is not in the "physical struggle" itself but in correct policies. But we call correct that policy which meets the conditions of the time and place. *By itself*, the workers' militia does not solve the problem. But the workers' militia is an *integrally necessary part* of the policy which meets the conditions of the time and place. It would be absurd to shoot guns over a ballot box. But it would be still more absurd to defend oneself against Fascist gangs with a ballot.

The initial nuclei of the workers' militia will inevitably be weak, isolated and inexperienced. Pedants and skeptics shake their heads with scorn. There will be found cynics who will not be ashamed to poke fun at the idea of workers' militia in a conversation with the journalists of the Comité des Forges. If they think thus to insure themselves against concentration camps they are fooling themselves. Imperialism has no use for the groveling of this or that leader; it must annihilate the class.

When Guesde and Lafargue, as youths, began to agitate for Marxism they appeared in the eyes of sage philistines to be impotent, solitary, and naive utopians. Nevertheless it was they who excavated the channel for that movement which carried along so many parliamentary routinists. Within the literary, trade union and co-operative spheres the first steps of the working class movement were feeble, tottering, very uncertain. But despite its poverty, the proletariat, thanks to its numbers and its spirit of self-sacrifice, has created mighty organizations.

The armed organization of the proletariat, which at the present moment coincides almost entirely with the *defense against Fascism,* is a new branch of the class struggle. The first steps here too will be inexperienced and maladroit. We must expect mistakes. It is even impossible to escape completely from provocation. The selection of the cadres will be achieved little by little and this all the more surely, all the more solidly, as the militia is closer to the factories where the workers know one another well. But the initiative must necessarily come from above. *The party can and must provide the initial cadres.* The trade unions must also take to this same road—and they will inevitably take it. The cadres will become fused and strengthened all the more rapidly as they meet with an increasing sympathy and increasing support within the workers' organizations, and afterwards within the masses of the toilers.

What are we to say about those gentlemen who, in the guise of sympathy and support, vilify and poke fun at or, worse yet, depict to the class enemy the detachments of working class self-defense as detachments of "insurrection" and of "putsch"? See in particular the "Combat (?) Marxiste (!)." The witty and half-witted pedants, the theoretical lieutenants of Jouhaux, led by the Russian Mensheviks, ridicule maliciously the first steps of the workers' militia. It is impossible to give these gentlemen any other name save that of direct enemies of the proletarian revolution.

* * *

But here the conservative routinists interject their final argument: "Do you really think that by means of squads of poorly armed militia of the proletariat you can conquer power, that is to say, win a victory over the army with its modern technique (with its tanks; aeroplanes! poison gases!!)?" It is difficult to conceive of an argument more hollow and trite, which, moreover, has been a hundred times refuted by theory and by history. Nevertheless it is served up each time as the last word of "realistic" thought.

Even if we allow for a moment that the detachments of militia will tomorrow turn out to be inept in the struggle for power, they are none the less necessary *today*, for the defense of the workers' organizations. The leaders of the C.G.T. reject, as every one knows, all struggle for power. This does not at all hinder the Fascists from annihilating the C.G.T. The trade unionists, who do not take timely defense measures, commit a crime against the trade unions, regardless of their political orientation.

Let us inspect more closely, however, the chief argument of the pacifists: "The armed detachments of workers are powerless against a contemporary army." This "argument" is aimed, fundamentally, not against the militia but *against the very idea of proletarian revolution*. Should one allow for a moment that the army equipped to its teeth will *under all conditions* be found on the side of big capital, then one must renounce not only the workers' militia but socialism in general. Then capitalism is eternal.

Fortunately, this is not so. The proletarian revolution presupposes the extreme aggravation of the class struggle in city and country and consequently also within the army. The revolution will not gain victory until it has won over to its side or has at least neutralized the basic nucleus of the army. This victory, however, cannot be improvised: it must be systematically prepared.

ONCE AGAIN, WHITHER FRANCE?

At this point the pacifist doctrinaire will interrupt us in order to express agreement (in words). "Obviously," he will say, "it is necessary to win over the army by means of sustained propaganda. But that is what we are doing. The struggle against the high death rate in the barracks, against the two-year term, against war—the success of this struggle makes needless the arming of the workers."

Is this true? No, it is fundamentally false. A peaceful, placid conquest of the army is even less possible than the peaceful winning of a parliamentary majority. Already the very moderate campaigns against the death rate in the barracks and against the two-year term are leading without any question to an understanding between the patriotic leagues and the reactionary officers, to a direct conspiracy on their part and also to a redoubled payment of the subsidies which finance capital gives to the Fascists. *The more successful the anti-militarist agitation becomes, the more rapid will be the growth of the Fascist danger.* Such is the actual and not fanciful dialectic of the struggle. The conclusion is that in the very process of the propaganda and of the preparation, we must know how to defend ourselves arms in hand, and more and more vigorously.

During the revolution, inevitable oscillations will occur in the army, an internal struggle will take place. Even the most advanced sections will not go over openly and actively to the side of the proletariat unless they see with their own eyes that the *workers want to fight and are able to win.* The task of the Fascist detachments will be to prevent the *rapprochement* between the revolutionary proletariat and the army. The Fascists will strive to annihilate the workers' insurrection at its outset in order to destroy among the best sections of the army any idea of the possibility of supporting the insurgents. At the same time the Fascists will come to the aid of reactionary detachments of the army to disarm the most revolutionary and the least "reliable" regiments.

What will be our task in this case?

LEON TROTSKY

It is impossible to tell in advance the concrete course of the revolution in any given country. But we can, on the basis of the entire experience of history, state with certainty that the insurrection in no case and in no country will assume the character of a mere duel between the workers' militia and the army. The relationship of forces will be much more complex and immeasurably more favorable to the proletariat. *The workers' militia*—not by its armaments but by its class consciousness and heroism—*will be the vanguard of the revolution. Fascism will be the vanguard of the counter-revolution.* The workers' militia with the support of the entire class, with the sympathy of all the toilers, will have to smash, disarm and terrorize the bandit gangs of reaction and thus open up the avenue to the workers for *revolutionary fraternization with the army.* The alliance of workers and soldiers will be victorious over the counter-revolutionary section. Thus victory will be assured.

The skeptics shrug their shoulders with scorn. But the skeptics have made the same gestures in the past on the eve of all victorious revolutions. The proletariat would do well to invite the skeptics to run away before things start. Time is too precious to explain music to the deaf, colors to the blind and the socialist revolution to skeptics.

5. The Proletariat, the Peasantry, the Army, the Women, the Youth

Jouhaux has borrowed the idea of the Plan from de Man. Both of them have the very same goal in mind; to disguise the final *collapse of reformism* and to instil new hopes in the proletariat, in order to sidetrack it away from revolution.

Neither de Man nor Jouhaux are the inventors of their "Plans." They merely took fundamental demands from the *Marxist program of the transition period*—the nationalization of banks and key industries—threw overboard the class struggle and in place of the revolutionary expropriation of

96

the expropriators substituted the financial operation of *purchasing*.

The power must remain, as previously, in the hands of the "people," that is to say, of the bourgeoisie. But the state purchases the most important branches of industry (we are not told which ones precisely) from their present proprietors, who become parasitic bond-holders for two or three generations: the pure and simple private capitalist exploitation is replaced by an indirect exploitation through the medium of state capitalism.

Since Jouhaux understands very well that even this emasculated program of nationalization is absolutely unfeasible without a revolutionary struggle, he announces in advance that he is ready to change his "Plan" into the small change of parliamentary reforms, after the manner of planned economy now in fashion. The ideal of Jouhaux would be to scale down the entire operation, by means of arrangements made behind the scenes, to the seating of the trade union bureaucrats in the different economic and industrial boards, without power and without authority, but with suitable fees.

It is not without good cause that Jouhaux's plan—his actual plan, which he hides behind the paper "Plan"—has received the support of the Neo-Socialists and even the approval of Herriot! However, the sober ideal of "independent" trade unionism cannot be materialized unless the working masses submit to bondage. But what if the capitalist decline continues? Then the plan, which was projected to sidetrack the workers away from "evil thoughts," can become the banner of a revolutionary movement.

Obviously frightened by the Belgian example, Jouhaux made haste to retreat. The most important point on the agenda of the National Committee of the C.G.T., in the middle of March—propaganda for the plan—was unexpectedly shuffled away. If this maneuver proved more or less successful, the blame for it falls entirely upon the leadership of the united front.

The leaders of the C.G.T. projected their "Plan" in

order to obtain the possibility for competing with the parties of the revolution. Thereby, Jouhaux has demonstrated that, following in the wake of his bourgeois inspirers, he estimates the situation as revolutionary (in the wide sense of the word). *But the revolutionary adversary has not appeared upon the arena.* Jouhaux decided not to involve himself further on a course which is full of risks. He retreated, and today he is biding his time.

In January, the Central Committee of the Socialist Party proposed to the Communist Party a joint struggle for power under the slogan of the socialization of banks and heavy industry. Had there been revolutionists seated in the Central Committee of the Communist Party, they would have grabbed this proposal with both hands. By opening a large scale campaign for power, they would have accelerated the revolutionary mobilization within the S.F.I.O., and at the same time they would have compelled Jouhaux to carry on an agitation for his "Plan." By following this course, the C.G.T. could have been forced to take its place in the United Front. The specific weight of the French proletariat would have increased greatly.

But within the Central Committee of the Communist Party preside not revolutionists but mandarins. "There is no revolutionary situation," they responded, contemplating their navels. The reformists of the S.F.I.O. sighed with relief—the danger was over. Jouhaux made haste to withdraw from the agenda the question of propaganda for the plan. The proletariat remains in a great social crisis *without any program.* The Communist International has played a reactionary role once again.

* * *

The crisis of agriculture provides today the principal reservoir for the Bonapartist and Fascist tendencies. When misery seizes the peasant by the throat he is capable of turning the most unexpected somersaults. He views democracy with a growing distrust.

"The slogan of the defense of democratic liberties,"

wrote Monmousseau (*Cahiers du Bolchevisme*, September 1, 1934, page 1017), "perfectly suits the spirit of the peasantry." This remarkable assertion demonstrates that Monmousseau understands as little concerning the peasant question as he does concerning the trade union question. The peasants are beginning to turn their backs to the parties of the "Left" precisely because the latter are incapable of proposing anything to them except frothy phrases about "the defense of democracy."

No program of "immediate demands" can give any serious results to the village. The proletariat must speak the *language of the revolution to the peasants*: it will not find another language in common. The workers must draw up a program of *revolutionary measures for the salvation of agriculture jointly with the peasants*.

The peasants dread *war* above all. Should we, perhaps, together with Laval and Litvinov delude them with hopes in a League of Nations and in "disarmament"? The only way to escape war is by overthrowing one's own bourgeoisie and by sounding the signal for the transformation of Europe into the *United States of Workers' and Peasants' Republics*. Outside of revolution, there is no safety from war.

The toiling peasants are overwhelmed by the usurious terms of credit. There is only one way to change these conditions: expropriate the banks, concentrate them in the hands of the workers' state and, at the expense of the financial sharks, provide *credit* to small peasants and to peasant co-operatives in particular. *Peasant control* must be established over agricultural banks of credit.

The peasants are subjected to the exploitation of the fertilizer and grain trusts. There is no way out other than the *nationalization* of fertilizer trusts and the big flour mills, and of subordinating them completely to the interests of peasants and consumers.

The various strata of the peasantry (the tenant farmers and the sharecroppers) are crushed beneath the exploitation of the great landed proprietors. There is no method of

struggle against *landed usury* other than the expropriation
of the landed usurers by *peasants' committees* under the
control of the workers' and peasants' State.

None of these measures is realizable under the rule of the
bourgeoisie. Meager charity will not save the peasant, he
has no use for palliatives. He needs bold revolutionary
measures. The peasant will understand them, approve them
and support them, if the worker makes him a serious proposal to *struggle jointly* for power.

We must not wait for the petty bourgeoisie to decide for
itself but we must *mold its opinions, strengthen its will*—
that is the task of the working class party. It is solely in
this that the union of workers and peasants can be achieved.

* * *

The mood of the majority of the army officers reflects
the reactionary mood of the ruling classes of the country,
but in a much more concentrated form. The mood of the
mass of the soldiery reflects the mood of the workers and
peasants, but in a much weaker form: the bourgeoisie knows
much better how to maintain contact with the officers than
the proletariat with the soldiers.

Fascism impresses the officers very much, because its slogans are resolute and because it is prepared to settle difficult questions by means of pistols and machine guns. We
have quite a few disjointed reports regarding the tie-up
between the Fascist leagues and the army through the medium of reserve as well as active officers, yet we obtain know-
ledge only of a minute portion of what is going on in reality.
Today the rule of re-enlisted men in the army is growing.
In them the reaction will find quite a number of supple-
mentary agents. *The Fascist nucleus of the army under
the protection of the General Staff is marching ahead.*

The young class-conscious workers in the barracks could
put up a successful resistance to the demoralizing Fascist
influence. But the great misfortune is that they are themselves politically disarmed: they have no program. The un-

employed youth, the son of a small peasant, of a small trader or of a petty functionary, carry into the army the discontent of the social strata from which they come. What will the Communist in the barracks say to them—"the situation is not revolutionary"? The Fascists pillage the Marxist program, successfully transforming certain of its sections into an instrument of social demagogy. The "Communists" (?) as a matter of fact, disown their own program, substituting for it the rotten refuse of reformism. Can one conceive of a more fraudulent bankruptcy?

L'Humanité concentrates upon "the immediate demands" of the soldiers: that is necessary but that is only one one-hundredth of the program. Today more than ever before the army lives a political life. Every social crisis is necessarily a crisis in the army. *The French soldier is waiting and seeking for clear answers. There is not and there cannot be* a better answer to the questions of the social crisis and a better rejoinder to the demagogy of the Fascists than the *program of Socialism*. It is necessary to spread it boldly throughout the country, and it will penetrate through a thousand channels into the army!

* * *

The social crisis, with its train of calamities, weighs most heavily upon the toiling women. They are doubly oppressed: by the possessing class and by their own families.

There are to be found "socialists" who dread giving the women the right to vote, in view of the influence which the Church has upon them. As if the fate of the people depended upon a lesser or greater number of municipalities of the "Left" in 1935, and not upon the moral, social and political position of millions of workers and peasants during the next period!

Every revolutionary crisis is characterized by the awakening of the best qualities in the women of the toiling classes: their passion, their heroism, their devotion. The influence of the Church will be swept away not by the impo-

LEON TROTSKY

tent rationalism of the "free thinkers," not by the insipid
bigotry of the free masons, but by the revolutionary struggle for the emancipation of humanity and, consequently,
first of all, of the working woman.

The program of the socialist revolution must resound in
our time as the tocsin for the women of the working class!

* * *

The most terrible condemnation of the leadership of the
political and trade union working class organizations is the
weakness of the youth organizations. In the sphere of *philanthropy, amusements and sports,* the bourgeoisie and the
Church are incomparably stronger than we are. We cannot
tear away the working class youth from them except by
means of the socialist program and revolutionary action.

The young generation of the proletariat needs a political
leadership but not irksome guardians. The conservative
bureaucratism stifles and repels the youth. Had the regime
of the Young Communist League existed in 1848, we would
not have had the *Gavroche.** The policies of passivity and
adaptation reflect in a particularly disastrous fashion upon
the *cadres* of the youth. The young bureaucrats grow old
before their time: they master all sorts of behind-the-scenes
maneuvers, but they do not know the A B C of Marxism.
They embrace "convictions" upon this or another occasion,
depending upon the exigencies of the maneuver. Those
among us who participated in the last congress of the Seine
Alliance have seen plenty of this type.

It is necessary to pose the problem of the revolution in
its full scope before the working class youth. In address-
ing ourselves to the younger generation, we must know how
to appeal to its audacity and its courage, without which
nothing great has ever been achieved in history. The revolution will open the gates wide for the youth. The youth
cannot fail to be for the revolution!

* The nickname for the independent impetuous youngsters of
revolutionary Paris.—Tr.

ONCE AGAIN, WHITHER FRANCE?

6. Why the Fourth International?

ₐn its letter to the National Council of the Socialist Party, the Central Committee of the Communist Party proposed as the basis for unification "the program of the Communist International, which has led to the victory of socialism in the U.S.S.R., whereas the program of the Second International was unable to stand up to the tragic test of the War and resulted in the disastrous balance sheet of Germany and Austria." Revolutionary Marxists announced in August 1914, that the Second International had failed. All subsequent events have only confirmed this estimate. But in showing the incontestable bankruptcy of the Social Democracy in Germany and Austria, the Stalinists forgot to reply to one question: *what became of the German and Austrian sections of the Communist International?* The German Communist Party fell before the test of history as ignominiously as the German Social Democracy. Why? The German workers wanted to struggle, and believed that "Moscow" would lead them to battle; they were moving steadily to the Left. The German Communist Party was growing rapidly; in Berlin it was larger than the Social Democratic Party. But before the hour of test came, it was ravaged from within. The stifling of the interior life of the party, the wish to give orders instead of to convince, the zigzag policies, the appointment of leaders from the top, the system of lies and deception for the masses—all this demoralized the party to its marrow. When danger approached, the party was found to be a corpse. It is impossible to erase this fact from history.

After the shameful capitulation of the Communist International in Germany, the Bolshevik-Leninists, without hesitating a moment, proclaimed: the Third International is dead! There is no need to recall the insults that were thrown at us by the Stalinists in all countries. *L'Humanité*, even after Hitler's definitive victory, kept saying in issue after

issue: "There has been no defeat in Germany"; "Only renegades will talk about defeat"; "The German Communist
Party is growing by the hour"; "The party of Thälmann is
getting ready for the seizure of power." There is nothing
surprising in the fact that this criminal bombast in the face
of the greatest of historical catastrophes has still further
demoralized the other sections of the Communist International: an organization which has lost the capacity of learning from its own defeats is irrevocably condemned.

Proof was not long in coming. The Saar Plebiscite was,
we might say, an experiment expressly designed to show how
much confidence the German proletariat had left in the
Second and Third Internationals. The results are known:
facing the necessity of choosing between the triumphant violence of Hitler and the rotten impotence of the bankrupt
working class parties, the masses gave Hitler 90% of their
votes, and (if we leave out the Jewish bourgeoisie, certain
interested business men, the pacifists, etc.) probably no
more than 7% to the united front of the Second and Third
Internationals. *This is the combined balance sheet of reformism and Stalinism.* Alas for those who have not understood this lesson!

The working masses voted for Hitler because they saw no
other road. The parties which for decades had aroused and
organized them in the name of Socialism, deceived and betrayed them. That is the general conclusion that the workers came to. If the flag of the socialist revolution had been
raised higher in France, the Saar proletariat would have
turned its eyes to the West and would have put class solidarity above national solidarity. But, unfortunately, the
crow of the French cock did not announce a revolutionary
dawn to the people of the Saar. Under cover of the United
Front in France, there reigned the same policy of feebleness,
of indecision, of marking time, of lack of confidence that
lost the cause of the German proletariat. That is why the
Saar plebiscite is not merely a test of the results of the
German catastrophe, but *a formidable warning for the*

ONCE AGAIN, WHITHER FRANCE?

French proletariat. Disaster awaits the parties which slide
over the surface of events, lull themselves with words, hope
in miracles and allow the mortal enemy to organize without
hindrance, to arm, to occupy the advantageous positions
and to choose the most favorable moment for launching the
decisive blow!

This is the lesson of the Saar.

* * *

Many reformists and centrists (that is, those who hesitate between reformism and a revolutionary position) in
turning to the Left are now trying to move toward the Communist International: some of them, especially the workers,
sincerely hope to find the reflection of the October Revolution in Moscow's program; others, especially bureaucrats,
are merely trying to establish friendly ties with the powerful Soviet bureaucracy. Let us leave the careerists to their
own fate. But we say to those socialists who sincerely hope
to find a revolutionary force in the Communist International: you are cruelly deceived. You do not understand the
history of the Communist International, which for the past
ten years has been a history of errors, catastrophes, capi-
tulations and bureaucratic degeneration.

The present program of the Communist International was
adopted at the Sixth Congress, in 1928, after the crushing
of the Leninist wing. There is an abyss between the present
program and that with which Bolshevism achieved victory in
1917. The program of Bolshevism started with the point
of view that the fate of the October Revolution is inseparable from the fate of the international revolution. The
program of 1928, in spite of all its "internationalist"
phrases, starts with the perspective of the *independent building of socialism in the U.S.S.R.* The program of Lenin declares: "Without revolution in the West and in the Orient,
we are lost." This program, *by its very essence,* precludes
the possibility of sacrificing the interests of the world workers' movement for the interests of the U.S.S.R. The pro-

gram of the Communist International means in practice: the interests of the proletarian revolution in France can and ought to be sacrificed to the interests of the U.S.S.R. (more strictly, to the interests of the diplomatic deals of the Soviet bureaucracy). The program of Lenin warns: Soviet bureaucratism is the worst enemy of socialism; bureaucratism, which reflects the pressure of bourgeois forces and tendencies, can lead to a revival of the bourgeoisie; the success of the struggle against the scourge of bureaucratism can be assured only by the victory of the European and the world proletariat. Contrary to this, the present program of the Communist International states: socialism can be built independently of the successes or defeats of the world proletarian movement, under the guidance of the infallible and all-powerful Soviet bureaucracy; anything directed against the infallibility of the bureaucracy is counter-revolutionary and should be exterminated.

In the present program of the Communist International there are, of course, plenty of expressions, formulas, phrases, etc., borrowed from the program of Lenin (the reactionary bureaucracy of Thermidor and the Consulate in France used Jacobin terminology in the same way) but at bottom the two programs are mutually exclusive. In practice, indeed, the Stalinist bureaucracy long ago replaced the program of the international proletarian revolution with a program of Soviet national reforms. Disorienting and enfeebling the world proletariat by its policies, which are a mixture of opportunism and adventurism, the Communist International thereby likewise undermines the fundamental interests of the U.S.S.R. We are *for* the U.S.S.R., but *against* the usurping bureaucracy and its blind instrument, the Communist International.

We grant that the Communist Party even now is growing. This is not thanks to its policies, but in spite of them. Events push the workers to the Left. The Communist Party, in spite of its present opportunist turn, represents in their eyes the "extreme Left." The numerical growth of the

ONCE AGAIN, WHITHER FRANCE?

Communist Party carries with it no guarantee whatever for the future: the German Communist Party, as we said before, grew up to the moment of its capitulation, and even more rapidly.

In any case, the fact of the existence of two working class parties, which makes a policy of united front in the face of common danger absolutely necessary, likewise suffices to explain the aspirations of the workers for organic unity. If there were a genuine revolutionary party in France, we should be firm opponents of fusion with an opportunist party. Under the conditions of the sharpened social crisis, the revolutionary party, in a struggle against reformism, would unquestionably rally under its banner the overwhelming majority of the workers. The historical problem is not to unite mechanically all the organizations, which continue to exist as representatives of different stages of the class struggle, but to rally the proletariat in struggle and for struggle. These are two absolutely different and even contradictory problems.

But it is a fact that in France there is no revolutionary party. The ease with which the Communist Party—without the least internal discussion—went over from the theory and practice of "social Fascism" to a bloc with the Radical Socialists and the repudiation of revolutionary tasks for the sake of "immediate demands" demonstrates that the apparatus of the party is completely shot through with cynicism, and its membership disoriented and unaccustomed to thinking. It is *a diseased party*.

We have criticized the position of the S.F.I.O. openly enough not to need a repetition of what we have already said more than once. But it is nevertheless unquestionable that the revolutionary Left wing of the S.F.I.O. little by little is becoming the laboratory in which the slogans and methods of proletarian struggle are forming. If this wing fortifies itself and becomes hardened, it can become the decisive factor in arousing the communist workers. It is along this road alone that salvation is possible. On the other hand,

107

the situation will be irrevocably lost if the revolutionary
wing of the Socialist Party falls into the meshes of the
apparatus of the Communist International which smashes
backbones and characters, destroys the power of thinking
and teaches blind obedience; this system is frankly disastrous as a means of making revolutionists.

Some comrades will ask us, not without indignation,
"Would you be against organic unity?"

No, we are not against unity. But we are against fetish-
ism, superstition and blindness. Unity in itself solves
nothing. The Austrian Social Democracy rallied almost
the entire proletariat, but only to lead it to ruin. The
Belgian Labor Party has the right to call itself the sole
party of the proletariat, but that does not prevent it from
going from capitulation to capitulation. Only people hopelessly naive can hope that the Labor Party, which completely dominates the British proletariat, is capable of
achieving victory. What decides the issue is not unity in
itself but its actual political content.

If the S.F.I.O. should unite this very day with the Communist Party, that would not guarantee victory any more
than the United Front guarantees it: only correct revolutionary policies can bring victory. But we are ready to
grant that unification, under present conditions, would facilitate the regrouping and reorganization of the genuinely
revolutionary elements now scattered throughout the two
parties. It is in this sense, and in this sense only, that
unification would be a step forward.

But unification—let us be clear about this point—would
be a step backward, even a step towards the abyss, if in the
new party the struggle against opportunism were directed
in the channels of the Communist International. The
Stalinist apparatus is capable of exploiting a victorious
revolution, but it is organically incapable of assuring the
victory of a new revolution. It is conservative to its marrow.
Let us repeat once again: *the Soviet bureaucracy has as
much in common with the old Bolshevik party as the bu-*

reaucracy of the Directory and of the Consulate had with Jacobinism.

The unification of the two parties would not lead us forward unless there is a break with illusions, blindness and outright deception. The Left Socialists must have a heavy inoculation of Leninism in order not to fall victim of the disease of the Communist International. This, among other reasons, is precisely why we are following the evolution of the Left groupings so attentively and so critically. Some feel offended by our attitude. But we believe that in revolutionary matters the rules of responsibility are incomparably more important than the rules of etiquette. Likewise, we accept criticism directed against us, from a revolutionary and not from a sentimental point of view.

* * *

In a series of articles, Zyromski has tried to indicate the fundamental principles of the future unified party. This is a much more serious matter than repeating general phrases about unity in the manner of Lebas. Unfortunately, Zyromski, in his articles, has a reformist centrist tendency whose direction is not towards Leninism but towards bureaucratic centrism (Stalinism). This comes out clearly, as we shall show, in the question of the dictatorship of the proletariat.

For some reason or other, Zyromski, in a whole series of articles, repeats with especial insistence the idea (moreover pointing to Stalin as original source) that "the dictatorship of the proletariat can never be considered as an end in itself." As if there were somewhere in the world insane theoreticians who thought that the dictatorship of the proletariat was an "end in itself"! But in these odd repetitions there lurks an idea: Zyromski is making his excuses to the workers in advance for wanting a dictatorship. Unfortunately, it is difficult to establish the dictatorship if we begin by apologizing for it.

Much worse, however, is the following idea: "This dictatorship of the proletariat . . . must be relaxed and progressively transformed into workers' democracy in proportion to the extent of the development of socialist construction." In these few lines there are two profound errors in principle. The dictatorship of the proletariat *is set up against* workers' democracy. However, the dictatorship of the proletariat by its very essence can and should be the supreme expression of workers' democracy. In order to bring about a great social revolution, there must be for the proletariat a supreme manifestation of all its forces and all its capacities: the proletariat is organized democratically precisely in order to put an end to its enemies. The dictatorship, according to Lenin, should "teach every cook to direct the State." The heavy hand of dictatorship is directed against the class enemies: *the foundation of the dictatorship is workers' democracy.*

According to Zyromski, workers' democracy will replace the dictatorship "in proportion to the extent of the development of socialist construction." This is an absolutely false perspective. In proportion to the extent that bourgeois society is transformed into socialist society, the workers' democracy will wither away together with the dictatorship, for the State itself will wither away. In a socialist society, there will be no place for "workers' democracy," first of all, because there will be no working class; and secondly because there will be no need for State repression. This is why the development of socialist society must mean not the transformation of the dictatorship into a democracy, but their common dissolution into the economic and cultural organization of the socialist society.

We should not have spent time on this error if it had a purely theoretic character. As a matter of fact there hides behind it a whole political scheme. Zyromski tries to adapt the theory of the dictatorship of the proletariat (which, according to his own admission, he has borrowed from Dan) to the present regime of the Soviet bureaucracy. Moreover, he deliberately shuts his eyes to the following question: why is it that, in spite of the enormous economic successes of the U.S.S.R., the proletarian dictatorship has developed not towards democracy but towards a monstrous bureaucratism which definitely is taking on the character of a personal regime? Why is it that, "in proportion to the extent of the development of socialist construction," the party, the Soviets and the unions are strangled? It is impossible to answer this question without a decisive criticism of Stalinism. But this is exactly what Zyromski wishes to avoid at all costs.

However, the fact that an independent an uncontrolled bureaucracy has usurped the defense of the socialist conquests of the proletarian revolution testifies that we are confronted with a diseased and degenerating dictatorship which, if left to itself, will end not in "workers' democracy," but in the complete collapse of the Soviet regime.

Only revolution in the West can save the October Revolution from defeat. The theory of "socialism in one country" is false in every root and branch. The whole program of the Communist International is just as false. To adopt this program would be to throw the train of the revolution off the tracks. The first condition for the success of the French proletariat is the complete independence of its vanguard from the nationalist and conservative Soviet bureaucracy. Naturally, the Communist Party has a right to propose the program of the Communist International as the basis for unification: it could hardly offer any other. But revolutionary Marxists, who understand their responsibilities for the fate of the proletariat, must submit the program of Bukharin-Stalin to pitiless criticism. Unity is a magnificent thing, but not on a rotted foundation. The progressive task is to rally the socialist and communist workers on the foundation of the international program of Marx and Lenin. The interests of the world proletariat as well as the interests of the U.S.S.R. (they are not different) de-

111

mands the same struggle against Stalinism as against reformism.

* * *

The two Internationals, not merely the Second but also the Third, are tainted to the marrow. The proofs of history do not deceive. Great events (China, England, Germany, Austria, Spain) have given their verdict. From this verdict, confirmed in the Saar, no further appeal is possible. The preparation for a new International, resting on the tragic lessons of the last ten years, is on the order of the day. This mighty task is closely bound up with the whole progress of the proletarian class struggle, above all with the struggle against Fascism in France. To conquer the enemy, the vanguard of the proletariat must assimilate the methods of revolutionary Marxism, methods incompatible both with opportunism and with Stalinism. Will we succeed in fulfilling this task? Engels once wrote: "The French always take on new life at the approach of battle." Let us hope that this time we shall fully justify the estimate of our great teacher. But the victory of the French proletariat is conceivable only if from the fire of struggle there emerges a truly revolutionary party, which will become the keystone of the new International. This road will be the shortest, the most advantageous and the most favorable for the international revolution.

It would be stupid to say that success is assured. If victory is possible, defeat too, unfortunately, is not excluded. *The present policies of the United Front, like those of the two trade union organizations, do not facilitate but jeopardize victory.* It is completely clear that in the event of the crushing of the French proletariat its two parties will definitely disappear from the scene. The necessity for a new International, on new foundations, would then become evident to every worker. But it is likewise completely clear in advance that, in the event of the triumph of Fascism in France, the building of the Fourth International would encounter a thousand obstacles and would proceed with extreme slowness; and that the center of the entire revolutionary movement, from every indication, would be transferred to America.

Thus the two historical alternatives—victory or defeat for the French proletariat—lead equally, though with different rhythms, toward the road to the Fourth International. It is precisely this historical tendency that the Bolshevik-Leninists express. We are strangers to adventurism in any form. We are not talking about "proclaiming" in an artificial manner the existence of the Fourth International, but of preparing for it systematically. By the test of events, we must show and demonstrate to the advanced workers that the programs and methods of the two existing Internationals are in insurmountable contradiction to the requirements of the proletarian revolution, and that the contradictions will not grow less but will, on the contrary, continually increase. From this analysis flows the only possible general line: we must, theoretically and practically, prepare for the Fourth International.

* * *

In February there took place an international conference of several organizations belonging neither to the Second nor to the Third Internationals (two Dutch parties, the German S.A.P., the British I.L.P., etc.). Except for the Dutch, who have a revolutionary Marxist position, all the other participants represent different varieties—on the whole, conservative varieties—of centrism. J. Doriot, who attended the conference, wrote in his account of it: "At the time when the crisis of capitalism offers startling verification of the Marxist theses . . . the parties created in the name of Marxism, whether by the Second or by the Third Internationals, *have all failed in their mission.*" We will not linger over the fact that Doriot himself, in the course of a ten year struggle against the Left Opposition, helped to disintegrate the Communist International. In particular, we will not stop to recall the sad role played by Doriot in the matter of the Chinese revolution. Let us concern ourselves merely with the fact that in February 1935, Doriot understood and recognized the failure of the Second and Third Internationals. Does he conclude from this failure the necessity for preparing the New International? To suppose so would be failing entirely to understand centrism. Doriot writes on the question of the New International: "This Trotskyist idea was formally condemned by the conference." Doriot lets himself be carried away when he talks about "formal condemnation," but it is true that, against the two Dutch delegates, the conference *rejected* the idea of the Fourth International. In this case, what then is the real program of the conference? It is to have no program. In its daily work the participants in the conference put aside the international tasks of the proletarian revolution and think about them very little. But every year or so they hold a congress to soothe their hearts and to say: "The Second and the Third Internationals have failed." After having nodded their heads sadly, they break up. We had better call this "organization" a "Bureau for the annual celebration of a funeral service for the Second and Third Internationals."

These venerable people believe themselves to be "realists," "tacticians," even "Marxists." They do no more than to scatter around aphorisms: "We must not anticipate events . . ."; "The masses do not yet understand . . ."; etc. But why then do you anticipate events yourselves by declaring the bankruptcy of the two Internationals: the "masses" have not yet understood it? And the masses who have understood it—without your help—they . . . vote for Hitler in the Saar. You subordinate the preparation of the Fourth International to a "historical process." But are you not yourselves part of this process? Marxists must always be at the head of the historical process. Just what part of the process do you represent?

"The masses do not yet understand." But the masses are not homogeneous. New ideas are first assimilated by the advanced elements, and, through them, penetrate the masses. If you yourselves, lofty wise men that you are, understand the inescapable necessity for the Fourth International, what right would you have to hide this conclusion from the masses? Worse still: after having recognized the failure of the existing Internationals, Doriot "condemns" (!!!) the idea of the new International. What concrete perspective, then, does he give to the revolutionary vanguard? None! But this means to sow confusion, trouble and demoralization.

Such is the nature of centrism. We must understand its nature to its roots. Under the pressure of circumstances, centrism can go far in analysis, evaluation, criticism: in this realm, the leaders of the S.A.P., who led the conference about which we have been speaking, repeated scrupulously much of what the Bolshevik-Leninists said two, three or ten years ago. But the centrist stops short fearfully when faced with revolutionary conclusions. A family celebration of a funeral service for the Communist International? Why not? But preparation for the New International? No, indeed. . . . Much better to "condemn" Trotskyism.

Doriot has no position. And he doesn't want to have any. After his break with the bureaucracy of the Communist International, he might have played a progressive and weighty role. But up to now he has not even approached it. He casts off revolutionary tasks. He has chosen for his teacher the leaders of the S.A.P. Does he want to be enrolled permanently in the corporation of centrists? Let him understand that a centrist is a knife without a blade!

7. Conclusion

"Wait," "Endure," "Gain Time"—these are the slogans of the reformists, the pacifists, the trade unionists and the Stalinists. This policy thrives upon the idea that *time works in our favor*. Is this true? This is fundamentally false. If in a pre-revolutionary situation, we do not conduct a revolutionary policy, then time works *against us*.

Despite the hollow hymns sung in honor of the United Front, the relationship of forces has changed during the last year to the detriment of the proletariat. Why? Marceau Pivert has given a correct answer to this question in his article "All Things Wait." (*Populaire*, March 18, 1935.) Directed behind the scenes by finance capital, all the forces and all the detachments of reaction are carrying out an unceasing policy of offense, capturing new positions, strengthening them, and marching forward (industry, agriculture, the schools, the press, the courts, the army). On the part of the proletariat there are only phrases heard about taking the offensive; as a matter of fact, there is not even a defense put up. The positions are not being strengthened, but being surrendered without a battle, or are being prepared for surrender.

The political relationship of forces is determined not solely by the objective factors (the role in the productive process, numerical strength, etc.) but by subjective factors: the *consciousness of strength* is the most important element of *actual strength*. While from one day to the next Fascism raises the self-confidence of the declassed petty bourgeoisie, the leading groups of the United Front weaken the will of the proletariat. Pacifists, disciples of Buddha and of Gandhi, but not of Marx and Lenin, exercise themselves in preaching against violence, against arming, against physical struggle. The Stalinists preach basically the very same thing, invoking solely the "non-revolutionary situation." Between the Fascists and the pacifists of all shades, a division of labor has become established: the former strengthen the camp of reaction, the latter debilitate the camp of revolution. Such is the naked truth!

Does this mean that the situation is hopeless? . . . Not at all!

Two important factors militate against the reformists and the Stalinists. First: the fresh lessons of Germany, Austria and Spain are before the eyes of everybody; the working class masses are alarmed, the reformists and the Stalinists are embarrassed. Secondly: the Marxists have succeeded in posing in time the problems of the revolution before the proletarian vanguard.

We, Bolshevik-Leninists, are far removed from the desire to exaggerate our numbers. But the power of our slogans flows from the fact that they reflect the logic of the development of the present pre-revolutionary situation. At each stage events confirm our analysis and our criticism. The Left wing of the Socialist Party is growing. In the Communist Party criticism is stifled, as hitherto. But the growth of the revolutionary wing in the S.F.I.O. will inevitably open a breach in the deadly bureaucratic discipline of the Stalinists: the revolutionists of the two parties will extend their hands to one another in joint activities.

Our rule remains what it always was: *to say what is.* That is the greatest service that one can now perform for the revolutionary cause. The forces of the proletariat have not been expended. The petty bourgeoisie has not made its choice as yet. We have lost a good deal of time, but the last extensions of time have not yet been exhausted.

Victory is possible! Even more: *Victory is certain*—in so far as victory can be made certain in advance—provided only that: *we have the will to victory. We must aspire to victory, we must surmount the obstacles, we must overwhelm the enemy, knock him down and put our knee on his chest.*

Comrades, friends, brothers and sisters! The Bolshevik-Leninists summon you to struggle and to victory!

March 28, 1935

3

France at the Turning Point

THIS BOOK IS devoted to elucidating the methods of the revolutionary policies of the proletariat in our epoch. The presentation is polemical in nature, like the revolutionary policy itself. Once the masses have been won, the polemic against the ruling class turns, at a certain stage, into revolution.

Revolutionary policy has its theoretical basis in a clear understanding of the class nature of modern society, of its state, its laws and its ideology. The bourgeoisie operates with abstractions ("nation," "fatherland," "democracy") in order to cover up thereby the exploiting character of its rule. *Le Temps*, one of the most venal newspapers on the terrestrial globe, gives daily lectures to the popular masses of France on patriotism and altruism. Meanwhile, it is a secret to nobody that the altruism of *le Temps* itself is on the market at fixed international rates.

The first step of revolutionary politics is the exposure of bourgeois fictions which poison the consciousness of the masses. These fictions acquire a particularly malignant character when amalgamated with the ideas of "socialism" and "revolution." Today, more than ever before, the tone in the workers' organizations of France is being set by the manufacturers of such amalgams.

The first edition of this book played a certain role in the formative stages of the French Communist Party. At that time considerable evidence of this came to the author's no-

* Written as an introduction to the new French edition of *Terrorism and Communism.*—TR.

tice, and, incidentally, it is not difficult to find traces of it in *l'Humanité* up to the year 1924. During the twelve years that have since elapsed, a radical re-casting of values took place in the Communist International—after a number of feverish zigzags. Suffice to mention that this work is listed today among the proscribed books. In their ideas and methods, the present leaders of the French Communist Party (we are compelled to retain this name which is in complete variance with reality) do not differ in any principle from Kautsky, against whom our work was originally directed. They are only infinitely more ignorant and cynical. The relapse into reformism and patriotism that Cachin and Co. are now living through might itself have served as a sufficient justification for a new edition of this book. However, more serious motives exist: they are rooted in the profound pre-revolutionary crisis which is convulsing the regime of the Third Republic.

* * *

After a lapse of eighteeen years, the author of this book has had the occasion to spend two years in France (1933-1935); to be sure, only as an observer in the provinces, who, moreover, found himself under constant police surveillance. During this time, in the Isère Department, where the writer had to live, a minor and quite banal routine episode occurred, which, however, provides the key to French politics as a whole. In a hospital, owned by the Comité des Forges, a young worker, about to undergo a serious operation, took the liberty to read the revolutionary press (or, to be more precise, the press which he innocently accepted as revolutionary, namely: *l'Humanité*). The hospital delivered an ultimatum to the careless patient and, later, to four others who shared his sympathies: either they must renounce receiving the undesirable publications or they would be immediately thrown out into the street. Of course it availed the patients nothing to argue that clerical-reactionary propaganda was being carried on quite openly in the hospital. Inasmuch as only ordinary workers were con-

cerned, who had neither mandates as deputies nor ministerial portfolios to risk, but only their health and lives, the
ultimatum proved ineffectual. Five sick men, one of whom
was scheduled for an operation, were ejected from the hospital. Grenoble at that time was a socialist municipality,
headed by Doctor Martin, one of those conservative bourgeois, who generally set the tone in the Socialist Party, and
whose consummate representative is Leon Blum. The ejected
workers sought a champion in the mayor. In vain. Despite
all entreaties, letters and intercessions they failed even to
obtain an interview. They then turned to the local Left
newspaper *Dépêche,* in which Radicals and Socialists com-
pose an indivisible cartel. Upon learning that the matter
involved the hospital of the Comité des Forges, the director
of the newspaper refused point blank to intervene: anything
your heart desires, except that! For a previous indiscretion
in connection with this all-powerful organization, *Dépêche* had already been deprived of an advertisement, and
suffered a loss of 20,000 francs. In contrast to the proletarians, the director of the "Left" newspaper, like the
mayor, stood to lose something. They therefore refused to
engage in an unequal struggle, leaving the workers with
their diseased intestines and kidneys to their fate.

Once every week or every fortnight, the socialist mayor
disturbs the dim recollections of his youth by delivering a
speech on the superiorities of socialism over capitalism.
During elections, *Dépêche* supports the mayor and his
party. Everything is in order. The Comité des Forges maintains an attitude of liberal tolerance towards socialism of
this sort, which does not do the least harm to the material interests of capitalism. By means of an advertisement of
20,000 francs per year (so cheaply are these gentlemen
priced!), the feudalists of the heavy industry and banks
keep a large cartel newspaper in actual subjection. And not
the newspaper alone. The Comité des Forges apparently has
arguments, both direct and indirect, weighty enough for
Messrs. Mayors, Senators, Deputies, including the Social-

ists. Entire official France is under the dictatorship of finance capital. In the Larousse dictionary this system is called a "democratic republic."

It seemed to the Messrs. Left deputies and journalists not only in the Isère, but in all the departments of France that there would be no end to their peaceful cohabitation with capitalist reaction. They were mistaken. Long corroded by dry-rot, democracy suddenly felt the barrel of a gun at its temple. Just as the re-armament of Hitler—a coarse material fact—brought about a real upheaval in the relations between states, laying bare the vain and illusory nature of the so-called "international law," just so did the arming of the gangs of Colonel de la Rocque result in convulsing the internal relations of France, compelling all parties without exception to reform their ranks, to assume a different coloration and to effect regroupments.

* * *

Friedrich Engels once wrote that the State, including the democratic republic, consists of detachments of armed men in defense of property; everything else serves only to embellish or camouflage this fact. Eloquent champions of "Law," like Herriot or Blum, always became incensed at such cynicism. But both Hitler and de la Rocque, each in his own domain, have once again demonstrated that Engels is correct.

Early in 1934, Daladier was the presiding Minister by will of universal, equal, direct and secret suffrage. He walked around with national sovereignty in his pocket alongside of his handkerchief. But the moment that the detachments of de la Rocque, Maurras and Co. showed that they dared to shoot and to slash the tendons of the police horses, sovereign Daladier surrendered his post to a political invalid designated by the leaders of the armed detachments. This fact is of considerably greater importance than all the electoral statistics, and it cannot be erased from the pages of the most recent history of France, for it forecasts the future.

Assuredly, the course of the political life of a country cannot be altered by *every* group armed with revolvers, at any time. Only those armed detachments which are the organs of specific classes can play a decisive role under *certain* conditions. Colonel de la Rocque and his henchmen seek to insure "law and order" against convulsions. And inasmuch as law and order in France signify the rule of finance capital over the middle and petty bourgeoisie, and the rule of the bourgeoisie as a whole over the proletariat and the social strata closest to it, the detachments of de la Rocque are simply the armed pickets of finance capital.

This idea is not new. One can often run across it even in the pages of *le Populaire* and *l'Humanité*, although, of course, they were not the original formulators of it. These publications, however, speak only half of the truth. The other and equally important half consists of the fact that Herriot and Daladier with their followers are also an agency of finance capital; otherwise the Radicals could not have been the ruling party in France for a period of decades. If we are not to play the game of hide and seek, we must say that de la Rocque and Daladier both serve one and the same master. This does not mean to say that either they themselves or their methods are identical. Quite the contrary. They fiercely war against each other, like two specialized agencies each of whom has its own special secret of salvation. Daladier promises to maintain order through the exercise of the selfsame tricolor democracy. De la Rocque holds that outlived parliamentarianism must be swept away and replaced by an open military-police dictatorship. The political methods are antagonistic but the social aims they serve are the same. The historical basis of the antagonism between de la Rocque and Daladier—we use these names merely for the sake of simplicity in our presentation—is the decline of the capitalist system, its incurable crisis, its decay. Despite the constant triumphs of technology and the

LEON TROTSKY

explosive successes achieved by individual branches of industry, capitalism as a whole acts as a brake upon the development of the productive forces, engendering an extreme instability in social and international relations. Parliamentary democracy is indissolubly bound up with the epoch of free competition and free international trade. The bourgeoisie was able to tolerate the freedom of strikes, of assembly and of the press only so long as the productive forces were mounting upwards, so long as the sales markets were being extended, the welfare of the popular masses, even if only partially, was rising and the capitalist nations were able to live and let live. It is otherwise now. If we exclude the Soviet Union, the imperialist epoch is characterized by the stagnation or decline of the national income, a chronic agrarian crisis and organic unemployment. These phenomena pertain internally to the present phase of capitalism just as gout and arterio-scelerosis pertain to certain ages of man. To explain world economic chaos by the consequences of the last war is to lay bare a hopeless superficiality in the spirit of Caillaux, Count Sforza and the like. The war itself was nothing else than an attempt on the part of capitalist countries to unload the already impending crash upon the enemy's back. The attempt failed. The war only deepened the manifestations of collapse, which, in its subsequent development, prepares a new war.

Bad as French economic statistics are, and although they deliberately evade the problems of class contradictions, even these statistics are unable to cover up the manifestations of a direct social disintegration. Amid the general decline of the national income, amid the truly horrifying fall in the income of the peasants, amid the ruin of the little men in the cities and the growth of unemployment, the gigantic enterprises with a turn-over above 100 to 200 millions a year are doing a brilliant business. Finance capital is sucking the lifeblood from the veins of the French people, in the full sense of the term. Such is the social basis for the ideology and politics of "national unity."

124

Mitigations and flickers of better times are possible in the process of decline; they are even inevitable. They remain, however, purely episodic in character. The general tendency of our epoch imperiously drives France, in the wake of a number of other countries, to the alternative: either the proletariat must overthrow the utterly decayed bourgeois order, or capitalism, in the interests of self-preservation, must replace democracy with Fascism. How long can Fascism last? The answer to this question will be provided by the fate of Mussolini and Hitler.

The Fascists fired their guns on February 6, 1934 at the direct orders of the Bourse, the banks and the trusts. From the selfsame ruling summits, Daladier received the instruction to hand over power to Doumergue. And if the Radical Premier capitulated—with the pusillanimity that is generally characteristic of the Radicals—it was precisely because he recognized his own master in the gangs of de la Rocque. In other words: sovereign Daladier surrendered power to Doumergue for the selfsame reason that the director of *Dépêche* and the mayor of Grenoble refused to expose the abominable cruelty of the agents of the Comité des Forges.

However, the transition from democracy to Fascism carries with it the danger of social upheavals. Thence arise the tactical vacillations and differences among the summits of the bourgeoisie. All the magnates of capital are in favor of further strengthening the armed detachments, which can serve as safety reserves in the hour of danger. But what place should be allotted to these detachments even today? Should they be permitted immediately to assume the offensive or should they still be held in reserve as a threat?— These questions remain unsolved as yet.

Finance capital no longer believes in the ability of the Radicals to lead the petty bourgeois masses behind them, and by means of the pressure exercised by these masses to restrain the proletariat within the framework of "democratic" discipline. But finance capital is likewise uncertain of the ability of the Fascist organizations, which still lack a real mass base, to seize power and establish firm order.

The behind-the-scenes leaders have been instilled with the need for caution not by parliamentary eloquence but by the rage of the workers, by the attempt of the General Strike, which, to be sure, was stifled at its very inception by the bureaucracy of Jouhaux and, later, by the local uprisings (Toulon, Brest . . .). A slight curb was placed on the Fascists, and the Radicals breathed just a bit easier. *Le Temps*, which had already rushed to offer its hand and heart in a number of articles to the "young generation," discovered anew the superior merits of a liberal regime, as the one most in harmony with French genius. Thus, the unstable, transitional, bastard regime was established, which harmonizes not with the genius of France but with the decline of the Third Republic. What stands out most sharply in this regime are its *Bonapartist* traits: the independence of power from parties and programs, the liquidation of the parliamentary legislation by means of emergency powers, the rising of the Government in the guise of an "arbiter" above the struggling camps, i.e., factually above the nation. The Ministries of Doumergue, Flandin, Laval, all three with the invariable participation of the compromised and abject Radicals, represented minor variations of one and the same theme. Upon the inauguration of the Sarraut ministry, Leon Blum, whose perspicacity possesses two dimensions instead of three, proclaimed that: "The final effects of February 6 have been destroyed on the parliamentary plane." (*Le Populaire*, Feb. 2, 1936.) This is commonly known as cleaning the shadow of a carriage with the shadow of a brush. As if it is possible, in general, to abolish "on the parliamentary plane" the pressure of the armed detachments of finance capital! As if Sarraut can escape feeling this pressure and not quake before it! In point of fact, the Sarraut-Flandin Government represents another variation of the selfsame semi-parliamentary "Bonapartism," only somewhat inclined to the "Left." Sarraut, himself, in replying to the charge of his having resorted to arbitrary measures gave the Chamber the best answer possible. Said Sarraut: "If my measures are arbitrary, it is because I aim to be an arbiter." This aphorism would not have sounded badly even on the lips of Napoleon III. Sarraut feels himself to be not the plenipotentiary of a certain party or a bloc of parties in power, as is in accordance with the rules of parliamentarianism, but an arbiter over classes and parties, as is in accordance with the laws of Bonapartism.

* * *

The sharpening of the class struggle, and especially the open emergence of the armed gangs of reaction, caused a similar upheaval among the workers' organizations. The Socialist Party which had been peacefully performing the role of the spare wheel in the chariot of the Third Republic, found itself compelled to half-renounce its cartel tradition, and even to break with its own Right wing (the Neos). Concurrently, the Communists completed their evolution in just the opposite direction, but on a scale infinitely more extensive. Over a period of several years these gentlemen had raved deliriously about barricades, conquering the streets, and so on (their delirium, to be sure, remained primarily literary in nature). Now after February 6, 1934, realizing that the situation had taken a serious turn, the specialists in barricades scurried to the Right. The normal reflex action of the scared phrasemongers coincided most propitiously with the new international orientation of Soviet diplomacy.

Oppressed by the danger threatening from Hitler Germany, the policy of the Kremlin turned towards France. Status quo—in international relations! Status quo—in the internal relations of the French regime! Hopes for the social revolution? Chimeras! The leading circles in the Kremlin refer as a rule only with contempt to French communism. One must hang on to what exists, lest things get worse. Parliamentary democracy in France is inconceivable without the Radicals: they must be supported by the Socialists. It is necessary to order the Communists not to hinder the bloc between Blum and Herriot and, if possible, the Communists, themselves, must join the bloc. No convulsions, no threats! Such is the course pursued by the Kremlin.

When Stalin renounces the world revolution, the bourgeois parties of France refuse to believe him. Needless caution! In politics, blind credulity is, of course, not a great virtue. But blind distrust is no better. One must know how to compare words with deeds and be able to recognize a general tendency of development over a period of years. The policy of Stalin, determined by the interests of the privileged Soviet bureaucracy, has become conservative through and through. The French bourgeoisie has ample reasons to place faith in Stalin. All the less reason for trust on the part of the French proletariat.

During the Trade Union Unity Congress at Toulouse, the "communist" Racamond gave a truly immortal formula of the policy of the People's Front: "How to overcome the timidity of the Radical Party?" How to overcome the bourgeoisie's fear of the proletariat? Very simply: the terrible revolutionists must fling away the knife clenched between their teeth, they must put pomade on their hair, and filch the smile of the most fascinating courtesan. The result will be Vaillant-Couturier—latest model. Under the onset of the pomaded "communists," who with all their strength pushed the Leftward moving Socialists to the Right, Blum had to change his course once again, fortunately, in the accustomed direction. Thus arose the People's Front—the society for insuring Radical bankrupts at the expense of the capital of the working class organizations.

Radicalism is inseparable from Freemasonry. When we say this, we have said everything. During the debate in the Chamber of Deputies on the Fascist leagues, Mr. Xavier Vallat recalled that Trotsky had once "prohibited" French Communists from participating in Masonic lodges. Mr. Jammy Schmidt, a high authority in this field, we believe, immediately explained this edict by the incompatibility between despotic Bolshevism and the "free spirit." We shall not enter into a dispute over this point with the Radical deputy. But we still consider that a labor representative who seeks inspiration or solace in the vapid Masonic cult of class collaboration is underserving of the slightest trust. It was not accidental that the cartel was supplemented by the extensive participation of the Socialists in the mummery of the lodges. Now the time has come for the repentant Communists also to don the aprons! Incidentally, the newly converted pupils will be able to serve the old masters of the cartel more comfortably in aprons.

But, we are told, not without indignation, the People's Front is not a cartel at all, but a mass movement. There is, of course, no lack of pompous definitions, but they do not change the nature of things. The job of the cartel always consisted in *putting a brake* upon the mass movement, directing it into the channels of class collaboration. This is precisely the job of the People's Front as well. The difference between them—and not an unimportant one—is that the traditional cartel was applied during the comparatively peaceful and stable epochs of the parliamentary regime. Now, however, when the masses are impatient and explosive, a more imposing brake is needed, with the participation of the "Communists." Joint meetings, parade processions, oaths, mixing the banners of the Commune and of Versailles, noise, bedlam, demagogy—all these serve a single aim: to curb and demoralize the mass movement.

While justifying himself in the Chamber before the Rights, Sarraut declared that his innocent concessions to the People's Front were nothing else than the *safety valve* of the regime. Such frankness may have seemed imprudent. But it was rewarded by violent applause from the benches of the extreme Left. There was no reason, therefore, for Sarraut to be bashful. In any case, he succeeded, perhaps not quite consciously, in providing a classic definition of the

People's Front: a safety valve for the mass movement. M. Sarraut is in every way fortunate with his aphorisms!

* * *

Foreign policy is the continuation of home policy. Having entirely renounced the viewpoint of the proletariat, Blum, Cachin and Co. adopt, under the screen of "collective security" and "international law," the viewpoint of national imperialism. They are preparing precisely the same policy of bootlicking which they had conducted in the years 1914 to 1918, adding only the phrase "For the Defense of the U.S.S.R." Yet during the years 1918-1923, when Soviet diplomacy was also obliged to veer considerably and to conclude a good many agreements, not a single one of the sections of the Communist International so much as even dared to think of a bloc with its own bourgeoisie! Is not this alone ample proof of the sincerity of Stalin's renunciation of the world revolution?

The selfsame motives which impelled the present leaders of the Comintern to suckle at the paps of "democracy" in its period of agony led them to discover the glorious image of the League of Nations, when the death rattle was already emanating from it. Thus was created a common platform of foreign policy between the Radicals and the Soviet Union. The home program of the People's Front is concocted of generalities which allow of as liberal an interpretation as does the Geneva covenant. The general meaning of the program is to leave everything as of old. Meanwhile, the masses refuse to accept the old any longer: therein lies the gist of the political crisis.

Disarming the proletariat politically, the Blums, Paul Faures, Cachins and Thorezes are most concerned lest the workers arm themselves physically. The agitation of these gentlemen does not differ in any way from the preacher's sermons on the superiorities of the moral principles. Engels who taught that the problem of state power is the problem of armed detachments, and Marx who looked upon insurrection as an art appear as medieval barbarians in the eyes of the present deputies, senators and mayors of the People's Front. For the one hundred and first time, *Populaire* prints a cartoon picturing a naked worker with the caption: "You will learn that our bare fists are more solid than all your blackjacks." What a splendid contempt for military technique! Even the Abyssinian Negus holds more progressive views on this subject. The overturns in Italy, Germany and Austria apparently do not exist for these people. Will they cease singing pæans to "bare fists" when de la Rocque claps handcuffs upon them? Sometimes one feels sorry that such an experience cannot be afforded privately to the Messrs. Leaders, without involving the masses!

From the standpoint of the bourgeois regime as a whole, the People's Front represents an episode in the competition between Radicalism and Fascism for the attention and good graces of big capital. By their theatrical fraternization with Socialists and Communists, the Radicals want to prove to the master that the situation of the regime is not as bad as the Rights assert; that the threat of the revolution is not at all so great; that even Vaillant-Couturier has swapped his knife for a dog collar; that through the medium of the domesticated "revolutionists" it is possible to discipline the working masses, and, consequently, to save the parliamentary system from shipwreck.

Not all the Radicals believe in this maneuver; the most solid and influential among them, headed by Herriot, prefer to take a watchful position. But in the last analysis they have nothing else to propose themselves. The crisis of parliamentarianism is first of all the crisis of the confidence of the voters in Radicalism. Until some method for rejuvenating capitalism is discovered there is not and cannot be any recipe for the salvation of the Radical Party. The latter has only the choice between two variants of political doom. Even the relative success it may score during the coming elections can neither avert nor even long postpone its ship-wreck.

The leaders of the Socialist Party, the most carefree politicians in France, do not burden themselves with the study of the sociology of the People's Front. No one can learn anything from the endless monologues of Leon Blum. As for the Communists, the latter, extremely proud of their initiative in the cause of collaboration with the bourgeoisie, picture the People's Front as *an alliance between the proletariat and the middle classes.* What a parody on Marxism! The Radical Party is not at all the party of the petty bourgeoisie. Nor is it a "bloc between the middle and the petty bourgeoisie," in accordance with the idiotic definition of the Moscow *Pravda.* The middle bourgeoisie exploits the petty bourgeoisie not only economically but also politically, and it itself is the agency of finance capital. To give the hierarchic political relations, based upon exploitation, the neutral name of a "bloc" is to make mock of reality. A horseman is not a bloc between a man and a horse. If the party of Herriot-Daladier extends its roots deeply into the petty bourgeoisie, and in part even into the working masses, it does so only in order to lull and dupe them in the interests of the capitalist order. The Radicals are the democratic party of French imperialism—any other definition is a lie.

The crisis of the capitalist system disarms the Radicals, depriving them of their traditional implements for lulling the petty bourgeoisie. "The middle classes" are beginning to sense, if not to understand, that it is impossible to save the situation through paltry reforms, that it is necessary to scrap audaciously the existing system. But Radicalism and audacity are as incompatible as fire and water. Fascism is fed above all by the growing lack of confidence of the petty bourgeoisie in radicalism. One can say without fear of exaggeration that the political fate of France in the period immediately ahead will take shape depending largely upon the manner in which Radicalism will be liquidated, and who will fall heir to its legacy, i.e., the influence upon the petty bourgeoisie: Fascism or the party of the proletariat.

* * *

The elementary axiom of Marxist strategy reads that the alliance between the proletariat and the little men of the city and country can be realized only in the irreconcilable struggle against the traditional parliamentary representation of the petty bourgeoisie. In order to attract the peasant to the side of the worker, it is necessary to tear the peasant away from the Radical politician, who subjects the peasant to finance capital. In contradistinction to this, the People's Front, the conspiracy between the labor bureaucracy and the worst political exploiters of the middle classes, is capable only of killing the faith of the masses in the revolutionary road and of driving them into the arms of the Fascist counter-revolution.

Unbelievable as it may seem, some cynics attempt to justify the policy of the People's Front by quoting Lenin, who if you please, proved that there is no getting along without "compromises" and, in particular, without making agreements with other parties. It has become an established rule among the leaders of the present Comintern to make mock of Lenin: they trample underfoot all the teachings of the builder of the Bolshevik party, and then they take a trip to Moscow to kneel before his mausoleum.

Lenin began his activities in Czarist Russia, where not only the proletariat, the peasantry and the intelligentsia but also wide circles of the bourgeoisie stood in opposition to the old regime. If the policy of the People's Front has any justification at all, one should imagine that it could be justified first of all in a country that has yet to achieve its bourgeois revolution. The Messrs. Falsifiers, however, would not do badly at all if they were to point out at what stage and under what conditions the Bolshevik party ever built even a semblance of the People's Front in Russia? Let them strain their imagination and rummage among the historical documents!

The Bolsheviks did conclude practical agreements with the revolutionary petty bourgeois organizations, for example, for joint illegal transport of revolutionary literature; sometimes to repulse the Black Hundred gangs. During elections to the state Duma they did, under certain conditions, enter into electoral blocs with the Mensheviks or the Social Revolutionaries, on the second ballot. That is all. No common "programs," no common and permanent institutions, no renunciation of the criticism of temporary allies. Such episodic agreements and compromises, confined strictly to practical aims—and Lenin never spoke of any other kind —have absolutely nothing in common with the People's Front which represents a conglomeration of heterogeneous organizations, a long term alliance between different classes, that are bound for an entire period—and what a period!— by a common program and a common policy, the policy of parades, declamations and of throwing up smokescreens. The People's Front will fall to pieces at the first serious test, and deep fissures will open up in all of its component sections. The policy of the People's Front is the policy of betrayal.

The rule of Bolshevism on the question of blocs reads: *march separately, strike together!* The rule of the leaders of the present Comintern is: *march together in order to be smashed separately.* Let these gentlemen hold on to Stalin and Dimitrov, but leave Lenin in peace!

It is impossible to read without indignation the declarations of the bragging leaders who allege that the People's Front has "saved" France from Fascism. In point of fact, they mean only to say that the mutual encouragement "saved" the scared heroes from their own exaggerated fears. For how long? Between Hitler's first uprising and his coming to power, a decade elapsed, which was marked by frequent ebbs and flows. At that time, the German Blums and Cachins also used to proclaim more than once their "victory" over national socialism. We refused to believe them, and we were not mistaken. This experience, however, has taught the French cousins of Wels and Thälmann nothing. In Germany, to be sure, the Communists did not participate in the People's Front, which united the Social Democracy with the bourgeois Left and the Catholic Center ("the alliance between the proletariat and the middle classes"!). During that period the Comintern rejected even fighting agreements between working class organizations against Fascism. The results are quite well known. The warmest sympathy to Thalmann as the captive of executioners cannot deter us from saying that his policy, i.e., the policy of Stalin, did more for Hitler's victory than the policy of Hitler himself. Having turned itself inside out, the Comintern now applies in France the quite familiar policy of the German Social Democracy. Is it really so difficult to foresee the results?

The coming parliamentary elections, no matter what their outcome, will not *in themselves* bring any serious changes into the situation: the voters, in the final analysis, are confronted with the choice between an arbiter of the type of Laval and an arbiter of the type, Herriot-Daladier. But inasmuch as Herriot has peacefully collaborated with Laval, and Daladier has supported them both, the difference between them is entirely insignificant, if measured by the scale of the tasks set by history.

To pretend that Herriot-Daladier are capable of proclaiming war against the "200 families" who rule France is to dupe the people shamelessly. The 200 families do not hang suspended in mid-air but are the crown of the system of finance capital. To cope with the 200 families it is necessary to overthrow the economic and political regime, in the maintenance of which Herriot and Daladier are just as much interested as Flandin and de la Rocque. The issue here is not a struggle of the "nation" against a handful of magnates as *l'Humanité* pictures it, but the struggle of the proletariat against the bourgeoisie. It is a question of the class struggle which can be resolved only by revolution.

The strikebreaking conspiracy of the People's Front has become the chief obstacle on this road.

It is impossible to say in advance how much longer the semi-parliamentary, semi-Bonapartist ministries will continue to succeed one another in France and in general through what concrete stages the country will pass in the next period. This depends upon the world and national economic cycle, upon the degree of stability of Italian and German Fascism, upon the course of events in Spain and last—but not least in importance—upon the awareness and the activity of the advanced elements of the French proletariat. The *dénouement* can be brought closer by the convulsions of the franc. A closer collaboration between France and England can postpone it. In any case the death-throes of "democracy" may drag out much longer than the pre-Fascist period of Brüning-Papen-Schleicher endured in Germany; but this does not stop it from being the death-throes just the same. Democracy will be swept away. The only question is: by whom?

* * *

The struggle against the "200 families," against Fascism and war, for peace, bread and freedom, and other magnificent things is either a lie, or it is the struggle for the overthrow of capitalism. The toilers of France are faced with the problem of the revolutionary conquest of power not as a distant goal but as the task of the coming period. Meanwhile, the Socialist and Communist leaders not only renounce the revolutionary mobilization of the proletariat, but resist it with all their strength. Fraternizing with the bourgeoisie, they hound and expel the Bolsheviks. So greatly do they hate the revolution and dread it! Under these conditions, the worst role is played by those pseudo-revolutionists of the type of Marceau Pivert who promise to overthrow the bourgeoisie, but only with the permission of Leon Blum! The entire course of the French labor movement for the last twelve years has placed the task of creating a new revolutionary party on the order of the day.

To speculate whether events will allow "sufficient" time for its formation is to engage in the most fruitless of all occupations. History has absolutely inexhaustible resources in the domain of different variants, historical forms, stages, accelerations and retardations. Under the influence of economic difficulties Fascism may venture prematurely and suffer a defeat. This would imply a long respite. Contrariwise, it may occupy a temporizing position too long and thereby increase the chances in favor of the revolutionary organizations. The People's Front may go to smash against its own contradictions before Fascism is able to engage in a general battle: this would signify a period of regroupments and splits in the parties of the working class, and a rapid fusion of the revolutionary vanguard. Spontaneous mass movements as in Toulon and Brest may attain a wide sweep and create a reliable fulcrum for the revolutionary lever. Finally, even the victory of Fascism in France, which is theoretically not excluded, does not mean that it will reign for 1,000 years as Hitler prophesies, or that it is even assured to endure as long as Mussolini has been able to maintain himself. Beginning with Italy or Germany, the twilight of Fascism would quickly spread over France as well. To build a revolutionary party in this, the least favorable variant, is to bring nearer the hour of vengeance. The wiseacres who shy away from the unpostponable task with the words, "the conditions are not yet mature," merely reveal that they themselves have not matured for the conditions.

The Marxists of France, as well as those of the entire world, must, in a certain sense, begin at the beginning, but on an infinitely higher historical level than their predecessors. Progress is at first rendered extremely difficult by the fall of the Communist International, more infamous than the fall of the Social Democracy in 1914. The new cadres are being recruited slowly, in a cruel struggle against the united front of the reactionary and patriotic bureaucracy in the working class. On the other hand, these very difficulties, which did not descend upon the proletariat accidentally, constitute an important condition for the correct selection and the firm tempering of the first detachments of the new party and the new International.

Only a very tiny section of the cadres of the Comintern began its revolutionary education from the outset of the war, prior to the October Revolution. All these elements, almost without a single exception, are now outside the Communist International. The next oldest stratum joined the already victorious October Revolution. This was much easier. But only an insignificant portion has remained even of this second draft. The overwhelming majority of the present cadres of the Comintern adhered not to the Bolshevik program, not to the revolutionary banner, but to the Soviet bureaucracy. These are not fighters but docile functionaries, adjutants, errand boys. It is by reason of this that the Third International is putrefying so infamously amid the historical situation so rich in great revolutionary possibilities.

The Fourth International rises on the shoulders of its three predecessors. It is subjected to blows from the front, the sides and the rear. Careerists, cowards, philistines have nothing to seek in our ranks. The percentage of sectarians and adventurists, inevitable at the beginning, is winnowed away as the movement grows. Let pedants and skeptics shrug their shoulders about "small" organizations that issue "small" papers and fling a challenge to the entire world. Serious revolutionists will pass contemptuously by the pedants and skeptics. The October Revolution also once began with its swaddling clothes. . . .

The mighty Russian parties of Social Revolutionaries and Mensheviks who made up the "People's Front" with the Cadets, crumbled into dust in the course of a few months under the blows of a "handful of fanatics" of Bolshevism. Subsequently the German Social Democracy, the German

Communist Party and the Austrian Social Democracy died an ignoble death under the blows of Fascism. The epoch which is drawing close for the European peoples will sweep out of the working class without leaving a trace all that is equivocal and rotten. All the Jouhauxs, Citrines, Blums, Cachins, Vanderveldes and Caballeros are only phantoms. The sections of the Second and Third Internationals will ingloriously leave the stage one after another. A new regroupment in the workers' ranks is inevitable. Young revolutionary cadres will gain flesh and blood. Victory is conceivable only on the basis of the methods of Bolshevism, to the defense of which this volume is dedicated.

March 26, 1936.

4

The Decisive Stage

THE RHYTHM OF events in France has become sharply accelerated. Hitherto the *pre-revolutionary* character of the situation had to be evaluated on the basis of a theoretical analysis and isolated political symptoms. Now facts speak for themselves. We may say without fear of exaggeration that in the whole of France there are only two parties whose leaders are unable to see and understand, or who refuse to see the full depth of the revolutionary crisis. They are the "Socialists" and "Communists." We ought, of course, to add the "independent" trade union leaders. The working masses are now creating a revolutionary situation by resorting to direct action. The bourgeoisie is in mortal fear of the development of events and, behind the scenes, under the nose of the new government, it takes all the steps necessary to defend and save itself, to dupe, to crush and to exact a bloody vengeance. The "Socialist" and "Communist" leaders alone continue to babble about the People's Front, as if their contemptible house of cards had not already been toppled by the class struggle.

Blum says: "The country has given its mandate to the People's Front and we cannot go beyond the limits of this mandate." Blum is duping his own party and he aims to dupe the proletariat. The Stalinists (they still continue to call themselves "Communists") assist him in this. As a matter of fact, the Socialists and Communists have utilized the dodges, snares and meshes of the electoral machinery to do violence to the toiling masses in the interests of an alliance with bourgeois radicalism. The political essence of the crisis lies in the fact that *the people are nauseated by the Radicals and their Third Republic.* The Fascists seek to profit from this. But what have the Socialists and Communists done? They have become the guarantors of the Radicals before the people. They have portrayed the Radicals as slandered innocents. They have assured the workers and peasants that complete salvation lies . . . in the ministry of Daladier. This was the leitmotif of the entire electoral campaign. How did the masses reply? By giving an enormous increase in votes and seats to the Communists, as the extreme Left. The masses have not yet understood the turns and zigzags of the hirelings of Soviet diplomacy because the masses have not yet tested them in their own experience. *The masses learn only in action, they have no time for theoretical studies.* When one and a half million voters cast their ballots for the Communists, the majority of them mean to say thereby: "We want you to do the same thing in France that the Russian Bolsheviks did in their country in October, 1917." Such is the real will of the most active section of the population, that section which is capable of fighting for and assuring the future of France. This is the first lesson of the elections.

Despite the split of the rather large section of the Neos, the Socialists have retained approximately their old number of votes. On this question, too, the masses gave their "leaders" a magnificent lesson. The Neos wanted a cartel at any price, i.e., the collaboration with the Republican bourgeoisie in the name of the salvation and the flowering of the "republic." Their split from the Socialists occurred precisely on this point, and they came out as competitors during the election. The voters turned their backs on them. The Neos have been crushed. Two years ago we predicted that the subsequent political development would in the first instance destroy all small groups gravitating towards the Radicals. In the conflict between the Socialists and the

Neos, the masses have condemned and discarded the group that was the most systematic and resolute, the loudest and the most outspoken in advocating an alliance with the bourgeoisie. Such is the second lesson of the elections.

The Socialist Party is not a working class party either with regard to its policies or its social composition. It is the party of the new middle estate (the functionaries, civil servants, etc.) and, in part, of the petty bourgeoisie and the labor aristocracy. A serious analysis of the electoral statistics would undoubtedly show that the Socialists lost to the Communists a considerable section of workers and poor peasants, while gaining from the Radicals, in turn, considerable groups of the middle classes. This means that the petty bourgeoisie is moving to the Left away from the Radicals, towards the Socialists and Communists, while groups of the middle and the big bourgeoisie are moving away from the Radicals to the Right. The regroupment is taking place along the class axes and not along the artificial line of the "People's Front." The revolutionary nature of the crisis is characterized by the rapid polarization of political relations. Such is the third, fundamental lesson.

The voter, therefore, has expressed his will—so far as he generally can in the strait-jacket of parliamentarianism— not in favor of the People's Front policy but against it. To be sure, on the second ballot the Socialists and the Communists further distorted the political will of the toilers by removing their candidates in favor of the bourgeois Radicals. Despite this, the Radicals emerged from the test with their ribs crushed, losing one-third of their seats. Says the *Temps*: "This is due to their entering into a bloc with revolutionists." Daladier retorts: "Without the People's Front we would have lost more." Daladier is absolutely right. Had the Socialists and the Communists conducted a class policy, i.e., fought for the alliance between the workers and the semi-proletarian elements in the city and country against the entire bourgeoisie, including its rotten Radical wing, they would have received many more votes, while the Radicals would have returned to the Chamber an insignificant group.

All the political facts prove that there is no basis for the People's Front either in the social relations of France or in the political moods of the masses. This policy is imposed from above: by the Radical bourgeoisie, by the Socialist business men and careerists, by the Soviet diplomats and their "Communist" lackeys. All together they have done everything possible by means of the most dishonest of all electoral systems, in order to dupe and rob politically the popular masses and to distort their real will. Nevertheless, even under these conditions the masses were able to give expression to their desire: not a coalition with the Radicals but the consolidation of the toilers against the whole bourgeoisie.

Had revolutionary working class candidates been run on the second ballot in all the electoral districts in which the Socialists and the Communists withdrew in favor of the Radicals, they would, no doubt, have obtained a very considerable number of votes. It is unfortunate that not a single organization was to be found capable of such initiative. This shows that the revolutionary groups both in the center and locally are lagging behind the dynamics of the events, and prefer to temporize and evade whenever it is necessary to act. This is a sad situation. But the general orientation of the masses is quite clear.

The Socialists and the Communists worked with all their might to prepare the ministry of Herriot—at worst, the ministry of Daladier. What did the masses do? They *imposed* upon the Socialists and the Communists the ministry of Blum. Is not this a direct vote against the policy of the People's Front?

Or, are more proofs necessary? The demonstration in memory of the Communards has obviously surpassed all the popular demonstrations witnessed in Paris this year. Yet the Radicals were not and could not have been connected in any way with this demonstration. The toiling masses of Paris, with an inimitable political instinct, have expressed their readiness to appear in redoubled force whenever they are not compelled to tolerate the repulsive fraternization between their leaders and the bourgeois exploiters. The mighty demonstration of May 24 is the most convincing and the most unalterable disavowal of the People's Front policy by working class Paris.

"But a parliament, without the People's Front and one in which the Socialists and the Communists would not have the majority anyway, would be a lifeless thing," and the Radicals—oh horror of horrors!—would be pushed into the "arms of reaction." Such reasoning is quite worthy of the cowardly philistines who are at the head of the Socialist and Communist Parties. The *lifelessness of the parliament is the inevitable consequence of the revolutionary nature of the crisis*. It was possible to disguise this lifelessness somewhat by a series of political frauds, but it will be exposed on the morrow just the same. In order not to push the Radicals, who are reactionary to the marrow of their bones, into the "arms of reaction," it is necessary to unite with the Radicals in defense of capitalism. This and this alone is the mission of the People's Front. But the workers hinder it.

* * *

The parliament is a lifeless thing because the present crisis opens no way out on the parliamentary road. Once again, the French toiling masses, with the fine revolutionary instinct that distinguishes them, have unfailingly seized upon this chief trait in the situation. In Toulon and Brest they sent up their first alarm signals. The protest of the soldiers against the *rabiot* (the increase in the service term) signified the most dangerous form of direct mass action against bourgeois order. Finally, during the days when the Socialist Party congress unanimously (together with that hollow phrasemonger, Marceau Pivert) accepted the mandate of the "People's Front" and entrusted this mandate to Leon Blum; in the days when Blum surveyed himself in the mirror from all sides, made pre-governmental gestures, issued pre-governmental exclamations, and commented upon them in articles which always have a great deal to say about Blum but never anything about the proletariat—precisely in those days the magnificent wave, a veritable Spring flood of strikes, rolled over France. Not finding leadership and managing to get along without it, the workers, boldly and with assurance, suspended work and occupied the factories.

Salengro, the new cop of capitalism, who has hardly had the time to assume power, hastened to proclaim (just as Herriot, Laval, Tardieu or de la Rocque would have done) that he would protect "order against anarchy." Order is the name that this person gives to capitalist anarchy. He gives the name anarchy to the struggle for a socialist order. The still peaceful occupation of mills and factories by the toilers are saying: "We wish to be masters in the buildings where until now we have been only slaves."

Mortally frightened, Leon Blum wants to scare the workers. He says: "I am no Kerensky; and even so, not Lenin would come to replace Kerensky in France but somebody else." One might imagine that the Russian Kerensky had understood the policy of Lenin or had foreseen his coming. In point of fact, Kerensky, to a hair like Blum, used to assure the workers that in the event of his downfall not Bolshevism would come to power, but "somebody else." Precisely there where Blum seeks to distinguish himself from Kerensky, he apes him most slavishly. However, it is impossible not to recognize that in so far as matters depend on Blum, he is really clearing the road to Fascism and not to the proletariat.

Most criminal and infamous in this situation is the conduct of the Communists: they have promised to give unswerving support to the Blum government, without entering it. "We are much too terrible revolutionists"—say the Cachins and Thorezes—"we might frighten our Radical colleagues to death. It is best for us to remain in the antechamber." Behind-the-scenes ministerialism is ten times more pernicious than the open and obvious variety. In point of fact, the Communists wish to preserve an outward semblance of independence in order better to subject working masses to the People's Front, i.e., to the discipline of capitalism. But here too the class struggle proves a hindrance. The simple and honest mass strike has mercilessly destroyed the mysticism and the mystification of the People's Front. The latter has already received its death blow; henceforth it can only die a lingering death.

There is no way out on the parliamentary road. Blum will not invent any gunpowder, because he is scared of gunpowder. The further machinations of the People's Front can only prolong the death agony of parliamentarianism and give de la Rocque time to prepare a new and more serious blow if . . . the revolutionists do not forestall him.

Following February 6, 1934, certain impatient comrades were of the opinion that the *dénouement* would take place "tomorrow," and that on this account it was necessary immediately to perform some sort of miracle. Such a "policy" could produce nothing but adventures and zigzags that have retarded in the extreme the growth of the revolutionary party. There is no regaining the time that has been lost. But no more time must be lost in the future, for very little time remains. Even today we shall not undertake to set dates. But after the great strike wave, events can unfold only either toward revolution or toward Fascism. That organization is unworthy of the name of revolutionary which will fail to find a base for itself in the present strike movement, which will prove unable to fuse itself firmly with the struggling workers. Its members had better seek room for themselves in the poor house or in the Freemason lodges (under the protection of Marceau Pivert)!

In France there are quite a few ladies of both sexes, ex-Communists, ex-Socialists, ex-syndicalists, who carry on a group or clique existence, exchanging impressions of events inside four walls, and who think that the time is not yet ripe for their enlightened participation. "It is still too soon."

When de la Rocque will have come, they will say: "Now it is too late." There is a considerable number of such thinkers, especially among the Left wing of the Guild of the Enlightened. It would be a great crime to waste even a spare moment upon these gentry. Let the dead bury their dead!

The fate of France is now being decided not in parliament, not in the editorial rooms of the conciliationist newspapers, both reformist and Stalinist, and not in the circles of skeptics, snivellers, and phrasemongers. The fate of France is being settled in the factories where the way out of capitalist anarchy has been shown in action. The place of revolutionists is in the factories!

The last Congress of the Comintern in its eclectic concoctions put the coalition with the Radicals side by side with the creation of mass Committees of Action, i.e., embryonic Soviets. Dimitrov, as well as his inspirers, seriously imagines that it is possible to combine class collaboration with the class struggle, a bloc with the bourgeoisie with the proletariat's struggle for power, friendship with Daladier with building of Soviets. The French Stalinists have renamed the Committees of Action People's Front Committees, imagining that by so doing they would reconcile revolutionary struggle with the protection of bourgeois democracy. The present strikes destroy this miserable illusion to its roots. The Radicals dread the strikes. The Socialists dread the fear of the Radicals. The Communists dread the fear of both. The slogan of the Committees can be realized only by a genuinely revolutionary organization, unwaveringly devoted to the masses, to their cause and their struggle. The French workers have once more shown that they are worthy of their historical reputation. We must have faith in them. The Soviets have always been born out of strikes. The mass strike is the natural element of the proletarian revolution. The Committees of Action cannot be at present anything but the committees of those strikers who are seizing the enterprises. From one industry to another, from one factory to the next, from one working class district to another, from city to city, the Committees of Action must establish a close bond with each other. They must meet in each city, in each productive group in their regions in order to end with a Congress of all the Committees of Action in France. This will be the new order which must take the place of the reigning anarchy.

June 5, 1936

The French Revolution Has Begun

NEVER HAS THE radio seemed so precious as during these days. From a distant village in Norway one can follow the pulse beats of the French revolution. Or rather, to put it more exactly, the reflection of these pulsations in the minds and voices of the Messrs. Ministers, trade union secretaries and other mortally terrified leaders.

To say "French revolution" may seem exaggerated. Oh, no! This is no exaggeration. That is precisely how a revolution springs into being. Generally speaking, a revolution cannot come into being any other way. The French revolution has begun.

To be sure, Leon Jouhaux, tailing Leon Blum, keeps assuring the bourgeoisie that this is a purely economic movement within the rigid framework of the law. The strikers, indeed, are seizing factories for the duration of the strike, establishing control over the bosses and their staffs. But one may shut one's eyes to this deplorable "detail." On the whole, these are . . . "craft strikes, not political strikes," the Messrs. Leaders keep repeating. Yet, under the influence of these "non-political" strikes the entire political situation in the country is being radically transformed. The government decides to act with haste it never thought of the night before. Indeed, according to Blum, true strength lay in patience! The capitalists are unexpectedly compliant. The entire counter-revolution bides its time behind the backs of Blum and Jouhaux. And this miracle is brought about

entirely by . . . "craft" strikes. What then would have
happened had the strikes been political?

Oh, no, the leaders are not telling the truth. The craft
union embraces the workers of a single, isolated trade,
separating them from other trades. Trade unionism and
reactionary syndicalism bend all efforts to keep the working
class movement within the framework of crafts. Upon this,
in fact, rests the dictatorship of the trade union bureaucracy
over the working class (the worst of all dictatorships!)
while the Jouhaux-Racamond clique in turn slavishly depends upon the bourgeois state. The essence of the present
movement consists precisely in that it is breaking through
trade union, craft and local bounds, raising beyond them the
demands, hopes and will of the whole proletariat. The movement takes on the character of an epidemic. The contagion
spreads from factory to factory, from craft to craft, from
district to district. All the layers of the working class seem
to be giving echoing answers to a roll call. The metal
workers begin—they are the vanguard. But the strength
of the movement lies in the fact that just behind the vanguard follow the heavy reserves of the class, including the
most backward trades, the rearguard, completely forgotten
on weekdays by Messrs. Parliamentarians and trade union
leaders. Not for nothing did *Le Peuple* openly confess that
the emergence of certain particularly low-paid categories of
the Paris population came to it as a complete "surprise."
Yet precisely in the depths of these most oppressed strata
inexhaustible springs of enthusiasm, selflessness and courage
lie hidden. The very fact of their awakening is the infallible
mark of the tidal wave. It is necessary to reach these layers
at all costs!

Tearing loose from the craft and local bounds, the strike
movement has become terrible not only for bourgeois society,
but also for the workers' own parliamentary and trade
union representatives who are primarily concerned with
closing their eyes to reality. Historical legend has it that

THE FRENCH REVOLUTION HAS BEGUN

Louis XVI, upon asking: "What is this, mutiny?" was answered by one of his courtiers: "No, sire, this is revolution." Now to the question of the bourgeoisie: "Is this mutiny?" its courtiers are replying: "No, these are only craft strikes." In giving comfort to the capitalists, Blum and Jouhaux are comforting themselves. But words will not help. To be sure, when these lines appear in the press, the first wave may have subsided. Outwardly life may seem to be returning to its old channels. But this changes nothing. These are not craft strikes that have taken place. These are not just strikes. This is a *strike*. This is the open rallying of the oppressed against the oppressors. This is the classic beginning of revolution.

The entire past experience of the working class, the history of its exploitation, miseries, struggles and defeats, comes to life under the impact of events and rises up in the consciousness of every proletarian, even the most backward, and drives him into the common ranks. The entire class has been set in motion. This colossal mass cannot be stopped by words. The struggle must be consummated either in the greatest of victories or the most ghastly of defeats.

* * *

Le Temps has called the strike the "practice maneuvers of the revolution." This is infinitely more serious than what is being said by Blum and Jouhaux. But even the definition given by *Le Temps* is incorrect, for it is in a certain sense exaggerated. Maneuvers presuppose the existence of a command, a general staff, a plan. This does not exist in the strike. The leading centers of the working class organizations, including those of the Communist Party, have been caught unawares. They are afraid, above all, lest the strike spoil all their blueprints. The radio relays a remarkable statement by Marcel Cachin: "We are all of us—we and the others—confronted by the fact of the strike." In other words, the strike is our common misfortune. With such words the terrible Senator persuades the capitalists to make

151

concessions in order not to aggravate the situation. The parliamentarians and the trade union secretaries, who are adapting themselves to the strike from the sidelines the sooner to extinguish it, stand in reality outside the strike, dangling in the air. They themselves do not know whether they will land feet or head first. The awakened mass is still without a revolutionary staff.

The ruling class has a real staff. This staff is not at all identical with the Blum government, although it uses the latter very skillfully. Capitalist reaction is now playing a big and risky game, but playing ably. At the present moment it is playing the game of "losers win." "Let us today concede all the unpleasant demands which have met with unanimous approval of Blum, Jouhaux and Daladier. It is a far cry from recognition in principle to realization in action. There is the parliament, there is the senate, there is the chancery—all these are instruments of obstruction. The masses will show impatience and will attempt to exert greater pressure. Daladier will divorce Blum. Thorez will try to shy to the Left. Blum and Jouhaux will part company with the masses. Then we shall make up for all the present concessions, and with interest." This is the reasoning of the real staff of the counter-revolution, the famous "200 families" and their hired strategists. They are acting in accordance with a plan. It would be light-minded to say that their plan is groundless. No, with the assistance of Blum, Jouhaux and Cachin, the counter-revolution *can* attain its goal.

The profound organic and genuinely revolutionary character of the strike wave is best of all characterized by the fact that the mass movement, though improvised, has acquired such vast scope and has exercised so great a political influence. This is the guarantee of the endurance of the movement, its stubbornness and the inevitability of a series of ever-rising waves. Without this, victory would be impossible. But all this is not enough for victory. As against the staff and the plan of the "200 families" there must be a staff and a plan of proletarian revolution. None as yet exist. But they can be created. All the prerequisites and all the elements for a new crystallization of the masses are at hand.

* * *

The sweep of the strike springs, we are told, from the "hopes" in the People's Front government. This is only one-quarter of the truth and even less than that. If matters were really limited to *hopes* alone, the workers would not have run the risk of struggle. The strike expresses above all the *distrust* or the *half-trust* of the workers, if not in the good intentions of the government, then in its ability to overcome obstacles and to come to grips with its problems. The proletarians want to "assist" the government, but in their own way, in the proletarian way. They still of course lack complete consciousness of their own strength. But it would be a gross distortion to portray matters as if the masses were guided only by pious "hopes" in Blum. It is not easy for them to muster their thoughts while yoked to the old leaders who try to drive them as soon as possible back into the old rut of slavery and routine. Nevertheless, the French proletariat is not at the beginning of its history. The strike has everywhere and in every place pushed the most thoughtful and fearless workers to the fore. To them belongs the initiative. They are still acting cautiously, feeling the ground under their feet. The vanguard detachments are trying not to rush ahead so as not to isolate themselves. The echoing and re-echoing answers of the hindmost ranks to their call gives them new courage. The roll call of the class has become a trial self-mobilization. The proletariat was itself in greatest need of this demonstration of its strength. The practical successes won, however precarious they may be, cannot fail to raise the self-confidence of the masses to an extraordinary degree, particularly among the most backward and oppressed strata.

That leaders have come forward in the industries and in the factories is the foremost conquest of the first wave. The elements of local and regional staffs have been created. The masses know them. They know one another. Real revolutionists will seek contact with them. Thus the first self-mobilization of the masses has outlined and in part brought forward the first elements of revolutionary leadership. The strike has stirred, revitalized and regenerated the whole colossal class organism. The old organizational shell has by no means dropped away. On the contrary, it still retains its hold quite stubbornly. But under it the new skin is already visible.

We do not speak now of the rhythm of events, which will undoubtedly be accelerated. In this sphere only suppositions and guesses are possible as yet. The second wave, its duration, its sweep and its intensity will doubtless permit a much more concrete prognosis than can be made now. But one thing is clear in advance: the second wave will not have by far the peaceful, almost good-natured, Spring-like character that the first has had. It will be more mature, more stubborn and harsh, for it will arise from the disillusionment of the masses in the practical results of the policies of the People's Front and their own initial venture. In the government a process of stratification will take place as well as in the parliamentary majority. The counter-revolution will immediately become more self-assured and brazen. Further easy successes cannot be expected by the masses. Faced with the danger of losing what seemed to have been won, faced with the growing resistance of the enemy and the confusion and indecision of the official leadership, the masses will feel the burning need of a program, an organization, a plan and a staff. For this we must prepare ourselves and the advanced workers. In the atmosphere of revolution the masses are swiftly re-educated, the cadres swiftly selected and tempered.

The revolutionary general staff cannot emerge from combinations at the top. The combat organization would not be identical with the party even if there were a mass revolutionary party in France, for the movement is incomparably broader than the party. The organization also cannot coincide with the trade unions for the unions embrace only an insignificant section of the class and are headed by an arch-reactionary bureaucracy. The new organization must correspond to the nature of the movement itself. It must reflect the struggling masses. It must express their growing will. This is a question of the direct representation of the revolutionary class. Here it is not necessary to invent new forms. Historical precedents exist. The industries and factories will elect their deputies who will meet to elaborate jointly plans of struggle and to provide the leadership. Nor is it necessary to invent the name for such an organization; it is the *Soviets of Workers' Deputies.*

The main section of the revolutionary workers is now following the Communist Party. In the past they have more than once cried: "Soviets Everywhere!" The majority of them undoubtedly accepted this slogan honestly and seriously. There was a time when we regarded this slogan as untimely. But now the situation has radically changed. The mighty collision of classes is heading towards a climax. Whoever vacillates, whoever loses time is a traitor. The choice lies between the greatest of all historical victories and the most ghastly of defeats. We must prepare for victory. "Soviets Everywhere"? Agreed. But it is time to pass from words to action.

June 9, 1936

GLOSSARY OF NAMES

BAUER, Otto — Austrian Socal Democratic leader. Foreign minister in coalition government after 1918 revolution. Follower of Kautsky. One of chief authors of the betrayal of the Austrian workers to Clerical-Fascist reaction.

BLUM, Léon — French Socialist Party leader. Premier at head of coalition government with bourgeois Radicals. Announced on taking office, June 1936, the necessity for remaining within the limits of capitalist order.

BRUENING, Heinrich — German Catholic Center Party leader. Chancellor of Germany, March 1930 to June 1932. Introduced first checks on Weimar constitution, ruling by decree laws. Replaced by von Papen. Party dissolved by Hitler. Now in exile.

CABALLERO, Francisco Largo — Spanish "Left-wing" Socialist. Advocates "dictatorship of proletariat" in words, opposes formation of Soviets in practice. Fancies himself the "Spanish Lenin." Tried to forestall Asturian insurrection October 1934, and was responsible for its isolation. Now playing a "Left" role in the Spanish People's Front.

CAILLAUX, Joseph — Radical Socialist. Ex-premier and finance minister. Now urging Blum government to devaluate the franc.

CHAUTEMPS, Camille — Radical Socialist. Minister of State in Blum cabinet. Premier, 1933-34. Retired in disgrace, Jan. 1934, in connection with the Stavisky scandals which involved him as Minister of Interior in previous cabinets. Later "exonerated."

CHIAPPE, Jean — Paris police prefect at the time of Feb. 6, 1934, Fascist riots. Now Nationalist deputy in Chamber.

CITRINE, Sir Walter — General Secretary of the British Trades Union Congress. Knighted for his services to British capitalism.

DEAT, Marcel — Neo-Socialist. Air Minister under Sarraut, January-June, 1936.

DALADIER, Edouard — Radical Socialist leader. Minister of Defense in Blum cabinet. Denounced by Socialists and Stalinists as an "assassin" at the time of the February 6 riots when he was premier. Capitulated at that time to the Fascists, giving way to the Bonapartist government of Doumergue. Welcomed into the fold of People's Front with whose help retrieved lost prestige. Touted as premier of future People's Front government

156

before the unexpectedly large gains of the Socialist and Stalinist parties in the May, 1936 elections forced Blum to take the helm. Occupies key position in Blum cabinet.

DAN, Theodore (Hourewitz, Theodore) — One of the leaders of the Russian Mensheviks. Editor of a number of Menshevik papers. Pacifist and centrist during the last imperialist war. After the downfall of Czarism—a defensist and conciliator; after the October Revolution active opponent of the Soviet state. At present in emigration, editing the organ founded by Martov, *Sotsialisticheski Vestnik*.

DE LA ROCQUE, François — Outstanding Fascist leader in France. Heads veterans' organization, Croix de Feu, which he merged with other nationalist, Right-wing bodies into the "Parti Social Français," June 1936, whose legality was recognized by Blum after the Croix de Feu had been "banned" as a semi-military organization. Spokesman for 1,000,000 followers. Openly proclaims intention to take power.

DE MAN, Henri — Belgian Socialist leader. Entered bourgeois cabinet of Van Zeeland as Minister of Public Works. Now Minister of Finance. Author of a plan to establish socialism by buying out the capitalists.

DEUTSCH, Julius — Austrian Social Democratic leader.

DUCLOS, Jacques — Stalinist deputy. Member Politbureau, French Communist Party.

DOLLFUSS, Engelbert — Clerical-Fascist Chancellor of Austria. Outlawed Socialist Party. Put down the workers by force, 1934. Anti-Nazi. Pro-Mussolini. Assassinated by Nazis, 1934.

DORIOT, Jacques — Former Stalinist bureaucrat. Expelled from Stalinist party for advocating a united front with the Social Democracy shortly before the Comintern adopted that policy in 1933. Now openly anti-Marxist and social patriotic.

DOUMERGUE, Gaston — Center politician. Ex-president of France. Called in to become the first Bonapartist premier in February 1934 after Daladier's capitulation to the Fascists. Ruled by decree. Tried to build an authoritarian regime. Replaced by Flandin, Nov. 1934.

FAURE, Paul — General Secretary of the French Socialist Party. Minister of State in the Blum cabinet. Blum's right-hand man.

FLANDIN, Pierre-Etienne — Center politician. Succeeded Doumergue as Bonapartist premier, making way for Laval May 1935. Foreign Minister under Sarraut, January-June 1936.

FROSSARD, Louis — Neo-Socialist. Minister of Labor under Sarraut.

GERMAIN-MARTIN, Louis — Center politician. Finance Minister under Doumergue and Flandin.

GRUMBACH — French Socialist, wrote under name of "Homo" in *l'Humanité* during the imperialist war.

GUESDE, Jules — One of the first French Marxists. Founded French Socialist Party together with Paul Lafargue. Co-author of its program. Opposed revisionism in Second International. Turned chauvinist, 1914, entering coalition government.

HERRIOT, Edouard — Radical Socialist leader. Ex-premier and foreign minister. Lukewarm to People's Front wooing. Consistently supported Bonapartist Laval as Minister of State. Saved from electoral defeat, May 1936, by Socialist-Stalinist support. Refused plea of Blum to take foreign portfolio. Elevated by Socialist-Stalinist votes to the presidency of the Chamber of Deputies.

HILFERDING, Rudolph — German Social Democrat; writer on economic subjects; author of the book *Finance Capital*. One of the leaders of the German Independent Social Democratic Party which adhered to the $2\frac{1}{2}$ International, and later returned to the Second International. Minister of Finance in the first coalition ministry of Stresemann.

JOUHAUX, Léon — Secretary of the C.G.T. (General Confederation of Labor) since 1909. Chief trade union bureaucrat. French equivalent of William Green.

JUST — French Socialist writer.

KUN, Bela — Hungarian Stalinist. Headed Hungarian Soviet Republic, March 1919. Emigrated to Austria after collapse of Hungarian Soviet August 1, 1919. Proceeded to Moscow where he now figures in Comintern councils.

LAFARGUE, Paul — Karl Marx's son-in-law. One of the founders of the Marxist movement in France.

LANGERON, Roger — Prefect of Police in Paris after Chiappe.

LAVAL, Pierre — Independent Center Republican. Foreign Minister under Doumergue and Flandin, 1934-35. Premier, June 1935. Ruled by decrees. Attempted deflation. Replaced by Sarraut, January 1936.

LEBAS, Jean-Baptiste — Socialist functionary. Minister of Labor under Blum.

LONGUET, Jean — Right-wing French Socialist. Founded, edited *Le Populaire,* Socialist organ. Voted war credits during the imperialist war.

MACDONALD, Ramsay — Ex-leader of British Labor Party. Prime Minister, 1924, 1929. Quit Labor to head "National" (Tory) government in 1931. Defeated for re-election in own constituency, 1935. Re-elected by a "safe" Conservative constituency. Betrayed British labor but achieved ambition of being kissed by duchesses. Retained as an ornament ("Lord President of the Council") in Baldwin cabinet.

GLOSSARY OF NAMES

MARIN, Louis — Extreme Right-wing deputy.

MARQUET, Adrien — Neo-Socialist. Minister of Labor under Doumergue.

MAURRAS, Charles — Editor of *l'Action Française,* French royalist organ.

MILLERAND, Alexandre — Social patriot. First Socialist to sit in a bourgeois cabinet. Quit Socialist Party, 1904. Together with other future "Socialist" ministers (Briand, Viviani) formed "Independent Socialist Party." Rewarded for services to French capitalism by election to the presidency of the Republic, 1920.

MONMOUSSEAU, Gaston — Stalinist trade union bureaucrat. Now an assistant to "Comrade" Jouhaux in the C.G.T.

MUELLER, Hermann — German Social Democrat. Foreign Minister under Gustav Bauer, 1919. Chancellor, 1927-29. Associate of Scheidemann and Noske. Succeeded by Brüning, 1930.

PAPEN, Franz von — Bonapartist Chancellor of Germany, heading a non-party cabinet succeeding Brüning, June 1932. Representative of East Prussian Junkers. Dissolved the Socialist goverment of Prussia. Succeeded by von Schleicher, December 1932. Advised Hindenburg to call in Hitler, under whom he became vice-chancellor. Now Minister to Vienna.

PAUL-BONCOUR, Joseph — Ex-Socialist. Often foreign minister and premier. Premier Blum's chief delegate to Geneva.

RACAMOND — French Stalinist trade union bureaucrat.

RENAUDEL, Pierre — Neo-Socialist-Democrat. Bonapartist premier replacing Laval, January 1936. Gave way to Blum, ·June 1936. Hailed People's Front as a defender of the "Republican order." Foreign policies supported by Socialist-Stalinist votes.

SALENGRO, Roger — Socialist Minister of the Interior under Blum.

SCHEIDEMANN, Philip — German Social Democrat. Together with Noske butchered German proletarian revolutionists. 1919-20.

SCHLEICHER, Kurt von — "Strong man" of German General Staff after Great War. "Power behind the throne" in Brüning, Von Papen cabinets. Took chancellorship from von Papen, December 1932. Ousted by Hindenburg to make way for Hitler, January 1933. Murdered by Nazis during "blood purge" of June 1934.

SCHMIDT, Jammy — Right-wing deputy.

SFORZA, Count Carlo — Italian diplomat. Ex-foreign minister.

TARDIEU, André — Right-wing leader. Ex-premier, minister. Last year openly abandoned parliamentary field, proclaiming its futility. Embarked upon extra-parliamentary political activity.

GLOSSARY OF NAMES

THAELMANN, Ernst — German Stalinist leader who led the C.P.G. to capitulation before Hitler. Now a prisoner of the Nazis.

VAILLANT-COUTURIER, Paul—French Stalinist leader. Editor of *l'Humanité*. Chief exponent of social patriotic line.

VALLAT, Xavier — Right-wing deputy. Active in Fascist leagues.

VIVIANI, René — Ex-Socialist. Entered Clemenceau cabinet as Minister of Labor, 1906. Entered Briand cabinet, 1909. Premier of National Defense Ministry during the war. Died 1925.

WELS, Otto — German Social Democratic leader. Capitulated to Hitler. Exiled anyway. Now in Czechoslovakia.

ZYROMSKI, Jean — French Socialist bureaucrat with strong Stalinist leanings.